Antitrust Policy
and
Vertical Restraints

Robert W. Hahn
editor

AEI-BROOKINGS JOINT CENTER
FOR REGULATORY STUDIES

Washington, D.C.

Antitrust Policy and Vertical Restraints may be ordered from:
Brookings Institution Press
1775 Massachusetts Avenue, N.W.
Washington, D.C. 20036
1-800/537-5487 or 410/516-6956
E-mail: hfscustserv@press.jhu.edu
www.brookings.edu

Library of Congress Cataloging-in-Publication data
Antitrust policy and vertical restraints / Robert W. Hahn, editor.
   p. cm.
Includes bibliographical references and index.
  ISBN-13: 978-0-8157-3391-1 (pbk. : alk. paper)
  ISBN-10: 0-8157-3391-7 (pbk. : alk. paper)
  1. Competition. 2. Commodity control. 3. Tie-ins (Marketing). 4. Monopolies. 5. Antitrust law.
I. Hahn, Robert W. (Robert William).
  HD41.A67 2006
  338.8'2-dc22   2006012580

9 8 7 6 5 4 3 2 1

The paper used in this publication meets minimum requirements of the American National Standard for Information Sciences—
Permanence of Paper for Printed Library Materials: ANSI Z39.48-1992.

Typeset in Adobe Garamond

Composition by OSP, Inc.
Arlington, Virginia

Printed by R. R. Donnelley
Harrisonburg, Virginia

Contents

Foreword

Businesses frequently engage in practices that may look anticompetitive on first blush but after some reflection turn out not to be so detrimental. One example might be the bundling of multiple features in what we have come to call a car. So, for example, a car is sold with a radio and windshield wipers even though some folks might not want the radio or might choose to replace the existing one with a different radio. The majority of consumers, however, are happy to get a car with a radio because it saves them time and trouble.

This book, at its heart, is really about examples like the car and the radio. It takes a hard look at business practices that may limit the options of purchasers or resellers in particular ways. It focuses broadly on the issue of "vertical restraints." Such restraints restrict the conditions under which firms may purchase, sell, or resell a good or service. In the car example, such restraints might require a dealer to sell the car with the radio and the wipers, or to meet certain standards for customer service in order to be a certified dealer of a certain brand. And, in exchange, a dealer may be given an exclusive territory in which he or she is the only franchised dealer.

The purpose of antitrust laws is to protect consumer welfare and foster competition. This means that policymakers need to understand which vertical restraints, under which specific circumstances, are likely to harm consumers more than they benefit competition. Then policymakers should try to limit only those practices that are likely to do more harm than good while leaving other more beneficial practices untouched. The question facing antitrust authorities is how to decide whether particular types of vertical restraints are likely to promote economic efficiency. This is not a simple task, and the government's record in this area is the subject of heated debate.

We asked a group of leading scholars to address the issue of vertical restraints in both theory and practice at a conference held at the AEI-Brookings Joint Center for Regulatory Studies on May 12, 2005. This collection of essays presents their analyses.

As the book reveals, the scholars hold diverse points of view. They all agree, however, that there are no one-size-fits-all solutions for issues involving vertical restraints. Vertical restraints are not always welfare enhancing nor are they always anticompetitive. In general, the scholars argue that the courts should consider vertical restraint issues on a case-by-case basis without assuming that practices, such as tying the sports page to the purchase of a newspaper, are illegal.

This volume is one in a series of books commissioned by the AEI-Brookings Joint Center for Regulatory Studies intended to clarify the issues in the continuing debate over antitrust policy. The Joint Center builds on the expertise of both sponsoring institutions on regulatory issues. The series addresses several fundamental issues in antitrust policy and regulation, including the design of effective reforms, the impact of proposed reforms on the public, and the political and institutional forces that affect reform. We hope that these publications will help illuminate many of the complex issues involved in designing and implementing regulation and regulatory reforms at all levels of government.

Like all Joint Center publications, this monograph can be freely downloaded at www.aei-brookings.org. We encourage educators to distribute these materials to their students by asking them to download publications directly from our website. The views expressed here are those of the authors and should not be attributed to the trustees, officers, or staff members of the American Enterprise Institute or the Brookings Institution.

ROBERT W. HAHN
ROBERT E. LITAN
AEI-Brookings Joint Center for Regulatory Studies

ROBERT W. HAHN

1 | *Introduction*

For some years, "vertical restraint" issues have been front and center in antitrust lawsuits. In the Department of Justice case against Microsoft, for example, one of the central issues was whether Microsoft's inclusion of Internet Explorer in the Windows operating system was an illegal tie, preventing personal computer manufacturers (and consumers) from choosing Netscape Navigator.[1] In another high profile case, Wal-Mart and other retailers accused Visa and Master-Card of illegally tying debit cards to the acceptance of credit cards, preventing retailers from defining their own payment policies. In a more recent case, Apple is being sued over allegedly tying its iTunes to its iPod players.[2] The company's iTunes music store, which offers individual songs for around one dollar each, puts those songs in a format that only works on its own iPod—not on much cheaper MP3 players.

Vertical restraints can be defined as any arrangement between firms operating at different levels of the manufacturing or distribution chain (the *vertical* part) that restricts the conditions under which such firms may purchase, sell, or resell (the *restraint* part).[3] For example, when manufacturers define

---

1. *United States* v. *Microsoft Corp.*, 84 F. Supp. 2d 9 (D.D.C. 1999) (setting forth findings of fact).
2. *Slattery* v. *Apple Computer, Inc.*, No. C 05-00037 JW, 2005 WL 2204981 (N.D. Cal. Sept. 9, 2005).
3. For a standard definition and discussion of vertical restraints, see Tirole (1997, chap. 4).

sales territories for their distributors so that each dealer has an exclusive area, or when contracts with distributors dictate that a dealer must sell one brand exclusively, those arrangements are considered vertical restraints. Both of these forms of exclusivity have pro-competitive as well as anticompetitive explanations. Limiting where and what products a dealer can sell can hinder competition by carving up a geographic market or by foreclosing competing product brands from a key distribution route. At the same time, guaranteeing a dealer that other dealers will not compete within a certain area provides the dealer with an incentive to promote the product, which can increase competition between products. Likewise, requiring brand exclusivity, so that dealers cannot sell competing brands, prevents rivals from free riding on a company's promotional and educational efforts. Such exclusivity is relatively common for products that require some degree of product knowledge on the part of the sales staff, such as with electronics and car parts.

Another common example of a vertical restraint is tying and bundling. With tying, a company only offers product A with the purchase of product B. Bundling is a similar but looser concept, where a company offers goods together in a bundle but also offers at least some of the goods separately as well. (So-called pure bundling is equivalent to tying.) Carmakers, for instance, bundle air conditioners, radios, tires, and more with the cars they sell. Nicer restaurants typically offer bread and water along with the items ordered, and word processing software includes a spell checker and a thesaurus.

Another vertical restraint is resale price maintenance. Under this arrangement a supplier sets a minimum or maximum price that limits the prices resellers distributing their goods may offer.[4] Suppliers may set prices in this fashion to maintain a reseller's profits and thus its incentives to distribute the good. A supplier may also set a maximum resale price in order to keep output at an optimal level to maximize its own profits.

Certain of these unilateral business practices, such as exclusive territories and tying and bundling, are quite prevalent in the economy. Given their widespread use, an understanding of their effects on rivals, competition, consumers, and the economy as a whole is important.

---

4. See Pepall, Richards, and Norman (1999).

The current focus on vertical restraints derives in part from changes in how the economics profession and the court view them. A few decades ago, legal opinion was almost uniformly hostile to all vertical restraints. The courts at the time argued that the only plausible goal for such restraints was to shut out competition.

Today, the courts are inclined to give such restraints the benefit of the doubt. The current view is that practices such as tying and exclusive contracts sometimes make markets more efficient, on balance benefiting consumers through lower prices and more rapid innovation. For example, as noted earlier, exclusive dealing, where a distributor is prevented from offering rivals' brands, can provide distributors with strong incentives to promote the manufacturer's brand and can prevent free riding on manufacturer advertising and support. Exclusive deals can also unduly deter competition, however, by preventing rivals from succeeding. The challenge lies in achieving a balance between the positive efficiency gains and the negative anticompetitive aspects of vertical restraints.

The purpose of antitrust laws is to protect consumer welfare and foster competition.[5] To achieve that end, policymakers should try to limit those practices that are likely to do more harm than good while leaving other more beneficial practices untouched. The question facing antitrust authorities is how to decide whether or not particular types of vertical restraints are likely to promote economic efficiency. This is not a simple task, and the government's record in this area is the subject of heated debate.[6]

Thus far, the academic literature has offered little guidance for achieving balance in the assessment of vertical restraints in practice. One line of thought, typically referred to as the Chicago School, maintains that abuse of monopoly power is not the reason for vertical restraints. According to this argument, a monopolist can exhaust its market power simply by raising prices to consumers, and thus any vertical restraints in place must be efficient and could not lower welfare.[7] This conclusion is based on stylized assumptions, however, including that the monopoly good is essential for the use of complementary goods and that the goods are consumed in fixed proportions. If you always need to use one unit of good A whenever you use one unit of

5. See Bork (1978).
6. See, for example, Crandall and Winston (2003); Baker (2003).
7. Hylton (2003, pp. 280–81).

good B, the firm selling A and B can collect monopoly rents either by charging more for good A *or* for good B—this is frequently referred to as the "single monopoly profit" theorem.

Challengers to the Chicago School have based their attacks on the underlying assumptions and conditions. For example, Salop and Scheffman find that vertical restraints can provide a means for firms to raise their rivals' costs and profitably reduce market output.[8] Whinston demonstrates that when the monopoly good is not essential for the consumption of complementary goods, then tying can indeed be profitable for a monopolist since it enables the firm to capture revenues from the sale of the complementary good when that good is used without the monopoly good.[9] While these theoretical models suggest that the conclusions of the Chicago School are open to question, they do not establish clear-cut rules for determining when vertical restraints are anticompetitive. Moreover, even when monopolists use vertical restraints for anticompetitive reasons, the welfare implications of the models are ambiguous.[10]

The empirical literature on vertical restraints can be useful for both informing theory and providing guidance for policymakers. Cooper and others observe that "there is a paucity of support for the proposition that vertical restraints/vertical integration are likely to harm consumers."[11] They review over twenty quantitative studies and find only one that claims to find clear evidence of harm to consumers, albeit at an extremely low level (specifically, a $0.60 per year loss for each consumer).[12] The majority of these empirical papers find positive effects from vertical restraints, primarily in the form of lower retail prices to consumers. Despite the general findings, though, it is difficult to apply the specific circumstances of one quantitative study to the particulars of a new court case.

The theoretical ambiguity over the benefits and costs of vertical restraints thus leaves antitrust policy in limbo. Two recent landmark cases, *United States* v. *Microsoft* and the decision by the European Court of First Instance to ban the GE-Honeywell merger, point to the urgency of coming to terms

8. Salop and Scheffman (1983, 1987).
9. Whinston (1990).
10. See Cooper and others (2005).
11. Cooper and others (2005, p. 648).
12. See the work of Ford and Jackson (1997), which studies vertical integration between cable television franchises and cable programmers.

with business practices that are widely used, especially in the ever-expanding high-tech industries. In the *Microsoft* case, the courts grappled with the distinction between anticompetitive tying and simple product design decisions, which firms should have the freedom to decide on their own. Adding Internet Explorer to Windows could have been a tie or it could have been a feature addition; the debate was heated over which interpretation was correct.[13] In the case of the GE-Honeywell merger, European competition authorities were concerned that the merged entity would be able to tie GE's jet engines with Honeywell's aerospace products to the detriment of rival companies and competition in aeronautics.

This volume presents three different perspectives on how policymakers ought to come to terms with vertical restraint practices. These perspectives are informed by both theory and practice.

The next chapter, by Bruce Kobayashi, a professor at George Mason University, helps explain why policymakers are still in need of guidance—even after decades of thought on vertical restraints. Kobayashi surveys the literature on one key vertical restraint practice: bundling. He finds that "the academic literature has focused on theoretically interesting uses of bundling that are likely to be of little empirical relevance. Little attention has been paid to the many well-known and obvious efficiency explanations for bundling."

Kobayashi pays particular attention to the literature on using bundling as a tool for exclusion. Combining goods into a single product can be helpful to consumers: in the car example mentioned earlier, carmakers add items that the majority of customers want anyway, and buying the goods together in a single package is more convenient. But bundling can also be used anti-competitively. In the early days of software, for instance, spell checkers were sold as stand-alone products. By incorporating a spell checker into a word processor, a word processor developer could foreclose a spell checker developer from the market. Of course, even when a competitor is excluded, the practice might still be viewed as efficiency enhancing if customers are better off. But Kobayashi argues that academic articles on tying typically start with an assumption of monopoly and market power and thus never explore the beneficial aspects of bundling when there is substantial competition.

---

13. *United States* v. *Microsoft Corp.*, 97 F. Supp. 2d 59 (D.D.C. 2000).

He concludes that until the literature gains a more nuanced understanding of the effects of bundling, "simple bright-line rules may dominate more complex tests that attempt to differentiate procompetitive from anticompetitive behavior." Kobayashi therefore encourages broadening the literature to study bundling practices among firms in competitive industries without any market power to provide a counterpoint to the studies emphasizing monopolies.

The third chapter assesses the issue from a different perspective. Dennis Carlton, a professor at the University of Chicago, and Michael Waldman, a professor at Cornell University, argue that one influential strand of the theoretical literature assumes too much in assigning pro-competitive motives to tying and bundling and thus misses important anticompetitive motives. In their chapter Carlton and Waldman explore a puzzle raised by the Chicago School. As explained above, the Chicago School maintains that a monopolist can only earn one monopoly profit (the single-monopoly profit theorem). Thus, under the conditions noted earlier, even if the firm produces other goods for competitive markets, it has no incentive to tie those goods to its monopoly profit since it cannot increase its profits.

What Carlton and Waldman ask is, if a monopolist does not need to tie an essential good in order to extract monopoly profits, why do we see real world monopolists tying essential goods to complementary goods? Here the authors have in mind the IBM antitrust cases of the 1970s and 1980s and the Microsoft trials of the 1990s and 2000s. These cases are examples of monopolists linking the purchase of an essential good (mainframe computers for IBM, the Windows operating system for Microsoft) to the purchase of a complementary good (peripheral equipment and Internet browsers, respectively).

After reviewing the antitrust cases, Carlton and Waldman conclude that the Chicago School theory is incomplete. They argue that monopolists do in fact have exclusionary reasons to tie essential goods. One such reason is to maintain a product as essential over time. Monopolists do not merely think of profit maximization today, but tomorrow as well. Thus IBM wanted its mainframe computers to remain dominant for multiple years, and Microsoft wanted its Windows operating system to keep its ubiquitous position in the market. The authors show that under certain conditions if rival firms face barriers to entry or if network effects are present (so that the number of people using a product today will influence how many want to use it tomorrow), then "the monopolist may tie in the first period in order to preserve its monopoly position in the second." In other words, tying two goods today is really a strategy aimed at tying purchases today with purchases in the future.

Other reasons Carlton and Waldman propose for monopolists to tie anticompetitively include instances where the good is durable (such as a car or a mainframe), where the good involves continuing revenue streams from upgrades (such as software), or when consumers find it difficult to switch from one brand of the good to another (think of software here as well). Again, the key point is that monopolists think about long-term profits as opposed to what they might simply receive in the short term. Profits can be increased if upgrade revenue streams can be captured or if consumers can be "locked in" to a good over time. Tying in these cases can also prevent rivals from expanding into a monopolist's core market, thereby maintaining the monopoly over time.

Despite the potential for anticompetitive motives, however, Carlton and Waldman do not advocate an interventionist policy. Acknowledging the many efficiency-based reasons for tying, along with the ambiguous social welfare implications even in the face of anticompetitive motives, the authors support high evidentiary rules for tying cases.

David Evans, a managing director at LECG, agrees that the evidentiary rules for tying cases should meet a high standard. In the fourth chapter, he argues that the antitrust rules on tying are in desperate need of modernization. Evans constructs four arguments in support of dropping tying as a per se violation—that is, of dropping the automatic assumption of illegality, regardless of the individual circumstances or the level of harm. First, he observes that "tying is an utterly common business practice in competitive markets." Since there can be no anticompetitive harm when firms have no market power, this observation implies that tying can be implemented for efficiency motives. In particular, tying can reduce company costs, save consumers money, and stimulate innovation.

Second, Evans argues that modern economics provides no support for per se illegality for tying. Tying is but one unilateral business practice, and it can be motivated by efficiencies *or* by anticompetitive goals. The only way to distinguish between the two is to evaluate each case, under a rule of reason. Following on this logic, Evans notes that the only thing holding the courts back from moving to a more lenient standard, such as a "rule of reason," is precedent. Under rule of reason, a practice is viewed with an open mind until proven anticompetitive, with the details of the case at hand determining whether the specific actions taken were on balance more harmful than beneficial. Some judges have been reluctant to abandon such a long court history of per se illegality, although others appear ready to make the jump. Finally, tying is only one of two unilateral practices by businesses (the other is minimum resale price maintenance) that is subject to a per se prohibition under the Sherman Antitrust Act. Other practices—even price fixing, thanks to the ruling in the BMI case that allowed some forms of price fixing as pro-competitive—have already moved to rule of reason.[14] These reasons, in Evans's opinion, stack up in favor of abandoning the per se violation status of tying.

While the authors represented in this volume differ in their opinions on how frequently vertical restraints are likely to result in competitive harm, they all agree on certain core issues. Most important, they agree that a move away from per se illegality toward a rule of reason standard for tying would allow for more careful analysis to inform decisions, increasing the chances that the courts could preserve welfare-enhancing business practices while extinguishing the more harmful ones. As part of that rule of reason approach, the authors all note that antitrust authorities should exercise good judgment, recognizing that economic theory leaves much to be desired in the real world of vertical restraints. Instead, the emphasis should be on the particular facts at hand, studied carefully through empirical analysis. These conclusions may not provide a simple handbook for policymakers, but they do provide sound advice on how antitrust authorities should proceed on bringing cases and on how courts should proceed in hearing them: slowly, carefully, and with an open mind.

14. *Broadcast Music, Inc.* v. *Columbia Broadcasting System*, 441 U.S. 1 (1979).

References

Baker, Jonathan B. 2003. "The Case for Antitrust Enforcement." *Journal of Economic Perspectives* 17, no. 4: 27–50.

Bork, Robert H. 1978. *The Antitrust Paradox*. New York: Free Press.

Cooper, James C., and others. 2005. "Vertical Antitrust Policy as a Problem of Inference." *International Journal of Industrial Organization* 23, nos. 7–8: 639–64.

Crandall, Robert, and Clifford Winston. 2003. "Does Antitrust Policy Improve Consumer Welfare?" *Journal of Economic Perspectives* 17, no. 4: 3–26.

Ford, George, and John Jackson. 1997. "Horizontal Concentration and Vertical Integration in the CableTelevision Industry." *Review of Industrial Organization* 12, no. 4: 501–18.

Hylton, Keith N. 2003. *Antitrust Law: Economic Theory and Common Law Evolution*. Cambridge University Press.

Pepall, Lynne, Daniel Richards, and George Norman. 1999. *Industrial Organization: Contemporary Theory and Practice*. Mason, Ohio: South-Western College Publishing.

Salop, Steven, and David Scheffman. 1983. "Raising Rivals' Costs." *American Economic Review* 73, no. 2: 267–71.

———. 1987. "Cost-Raising Strategies." *Journal of Industrial Economics* 36, no. 1: 19–34.

Tirole, Jean. 1997. *The Theory of Industrial Organization*. MIT Press.

Whinston, Michael D. 1990. "Tying, Foreclosure, and Exclusion." *American Economic Review* 80, no. 4: 837–59.

BRUCE H. KOBAYASHI

2 | *Two Tales of Bundling: Implications for the Application of Antitrust Law to Bundled Discounts*

B undling, or the selling of two separate goods in a package, is a ubiquitous phenomenon. Bundling is used by firms producing a wide variety of products and services, and is used to sell products at both the retail and wholesale level. Bundling is used by established firms and by new entrants, by dominant firms and by firms with many competitors, and by firms in both regulated and unregulated industries. The widespread and ubiquitous use of bundling by firms, especially by those in highly competitive markets, suggests that bundling yields widespread benefits for both firms and consumers.

Firms bundle for a wide variety of reasons. At the consumer level, bundling is used by firms to give selective discounts to consumers.[1] In this

The author acknowledges financial support from the Law and Economics Center at George Mason University School of Law. The author would also like to thank Bob Hahn, Tim Muris, and an anonymous referee for comments.

1. For example, airline websites encourage consumers to "save big by bundling" hotel and rental car reservations in a package with their airline tickets. Bundling is a major component of travel websites' strategy to compete with travel agents. For a discussion of the bundling used by Expedia.com, Orbitz.com, and Travelocity.com, see Missy Sullivan, "Vacation Wars," *Forbes.com*, March 20, 2003 (www.forbes.com/best/2003/0320/001_print.html).

Telecommunications companies also offer discounts to customers that bundle services such as unlimited local calling, call waiting and call forwarding, unlimited long distance, a digital subscriber line, and wireless phone services. See, for example, Ray Martin, "Save by 'Bundling,'" *CBSNews.com*, February 28, 2003 (www.cbsnews.com/stories/2003/02/28/earlyshow/contributors/raymartin/main542428.shtml).

context, bundling is an efficient form of competitive advertising that directly benefits consumers through lower prices on high-value promotional items.[2] Bundle discounts are also used by business as a way to facilitate entry into new markets. For example, cable companies are now attempting to compete with telecommunications companies by offering competing bundles that include digital telephone service, high-speed Internet service, and digital cable. Telecommunications companies have responded by offering discounts if consumers bundle their bundled phone service and DSL service with satellite television service. This bundle-versus-bundle competition is blurring the lines between these two once-distinct industries, and the resulting increase in competition has called into question the wisdom and viability of existing telecommunications regulations.

Bundling is also used as a way to reduce the transaction and information costs involved in purchasing, distributing, and selling goods and services. Bundling can enable firms to achieve economies of scale or scope in production and distribution, and can allow them to package and market integrated and compatible products to consumers. These transaction cost savings can explain the use of standardized option packages for automobiles, computer hardware and software, and the packaging of cold remedies and analgesics.[3] Bundling allows firms to offer a discrete number of standardized products to consumers and can serve to reduce consumers' and firms' search and information costs.[4]

Moreover, bundling can be used to reduce the divergence in incentives that exists between manufacturers and those who distribute their products. The provision of promotional and other point-of-sale services for a manufacturer's products at the retail level may be necessary for the manufacturer to increase the demand for its products and reach an optimal level of output. However, retailers will often have inadequate incentives to provide such promotional and point-of-sale services. The use of bundled rebates can ensure that distributors or retailers of a manufacturer's goods have strong incentives to promote and sell these goods. Bundled rebates can be used by manufacturers as a way to compensate retailers for their efforts on behalf of the manufacturer, thus serving to mitigate retailer free riding and hold-up

2. See generally Telser (1972), discussing the relationship of advertising and competition.

3. Evans and Salinger (2005).

4. Kenney and Klein (1983) discuss the block booking of films as a way to minimize search costs and to reduce the cost of distributing a standardized product.

problems. In this way bundled rebates can serve the same efficiency-promoting vertical control functions as have been identified in the literature examining the use of tying, exclusive dealing, and other forms of vertical restraints.[5] However, unlike exclusive dealing, use of bundled rebates does not prevent retailers from offering consumers other manufacturers' products. This difference is likely to be significant when retailers' point-of-sale services and consumers' demand for variety at the retail level are both important.[6]

In many cases where bundling is observed, the reason why separate goods are sold in a package is easily explained on efficiency grounds. This is certainly the presumptive explanation for bundling when it occurs in highly competitive markets.[7] These efficiency-based explanations also apply with equal force to the use of bundling by firms with market power.[8] In addition, firms with market power can use bundling for other reasons— for example, as a price discrimination device or a way to internalize pricing externalities in the presence of complementary goods.

However, in markets where firms can exercise monopoly power, bundling can have anticompetitive uses that may be scrutinized under the antitrust laws. There is a growing theoretical literature demonstrating how bundling can be used by monopolists to deter entry and exclude rivals. Indeed, if bundling can generate the same efficiency-promoting functions as exclusive dealing and tying, then it stands to reason that it also could promote the anticompetitive functions associated with such practices.[9] Because bundling can also be an efficient practice when firms possess market power, any rational antitrust evaluation of bundling must simultaneously consider both the strategic and efficiency reasons for its use.

This chapter examines two distinct parts of the voluminous economic literature on bundling as a first attempt to gauge how much is known about the relative costs and benefits of bundling. The first, the literature on bundling by a multiproduct monopolist, was chosen because the progression of the literature nicely illustrates several key methodological issues. Specifically, it illustrates how the academic literature on bundling reflects topic

5. For example, see Marvel (1982); Klein (2003); Heide, Dutta, and Bergen (1998).
6. See Klein and Wright (2005), noting a similar explanation for the use of category management, and Mills (2004), discussing similar use of loyalty or market share discount programs.
7. Evans and Salinger (2005, note 3); Evans and Padilla (2005).
8. Evans and Padilla (2005, note 7).
9. See generally Tom, Balto, and Averitt (2000); Gavil (2004).

selection determined by the interests of academic economists and not by an attempt to provide a representative or comprehensive explanation for bundling. As a result the academic literature has focused on theoretically interesting uses of bundling that are likely to be of little empirical relevance. Little attention has been paid to the many well-known and obvious efficiency explanations for bundling, largely because the obvious and transparent nature of such efficiency explanations makes them unlikely subjects for publishable academic articles.[10]

This chapter also examines the recent literature on bundling as an exclusionary device, an area chosen because of its potential relevance to current antitrust issues. While these papers present interesting results, they are underdeveloped in several important ways. These articles begin with the assumption of monopoly, explicitly ignore efficiency considerations in order to highlight the possibility of anticompetitive harm, and do not apply consistent welfare standards. Moreover, these papers are almost exclusively theoretical and contain many restrictive assumptions that have not been subjected to tests of robustness or to rigorous empirical testing.

Both areas illustrate the underdeveloped nature of the current literature. As a basis for guiding antitrust policy, the literature does not provide any reliable way to trade off the theoretical risk of exclusionary harm against the potential efficiency gains from bundling. As a result, when applied in practice, simple bright-line rules may dominate more complex tests that attempt to differentiate procompetitive from anticompetitive behavior. Improving the reliability of more complex tests for anticompetitive behavior will require economists to expand their understanding of both the anticompetitive and procompetitive reasons firms engage in bundling.

Academic Literature on the Economics of Bundling: Two Examples

The academic literature has defined bundling as the sale of two or more separate products in a package. Separate products are defined as those for which consumer demand exists for the stand-alone products outside of the

10. Evans and Salinger (2005, note 3). Moreover, there may be efficiency benefits from bundling that are less obvious. These, too, have been largely ignored by academics.

bundle. This definition of bundling can include the packaging of a fixed quantity of a single good as well as the packaging of two or more separate goods.

There are two basic types of bundling. The first type is *pure bundling*, where the firm selling the bundle chooses only to sell the package and not the stand-alone goods. The second type of bundling is *mixed bundling*, where the firm selling the package also sells the stand-alone goods. Bundling can be achieved via *price bundling*, where the bundle is sold at a discount (as in the bundling of a hotel, rental car, and airline ticket); *product bundling*, where the component goods are physically integrated to yield extra value to the buyer (for example, a high degree of interoperability in a computer operating system or a suite of office software); or a combination of the two.

While some authors define all types of pure bundling as tying, bundling has been distinguished from tying under the antitrust laws. The Supreme Court has defined tying to include those cases in which the seller conditions the sale of the tying good upon the buyer's agreeing to purchase the tied product from him.[11] Practices by firms with monopoly power that involve such coercion can be per se illegal. Bundling and other forms of packaged sales have generally been found to lack this coercive element.

The economic literature on bundling is voluminous and has a long history. Rather than attempt to comprehensively describe the literature, this section focuses on two distinct areas in which economists have studied the use of bundling.[12] The first is the literature on the use of bundling by a multiproduct monopolist. The second is the recent literature on the use of bundling as an exclusionary device. The former was chosen because it nicely illustrates many of the methodological issues described above. The latter was chosen because of its potential relevance to current antitrust issues.

Block Booking and the Multiproduct Monopolist

The most common explanation in the literature for bundling is price discrimination. This does not imply, however, that price discrimination is the most common reason firms engage in bundling.[13] Rather, it is the explana-

---

11. *Jefferson Parish Hospital District No. 2* v. *Hyde,* 466 U.S. 2 (1984).

12. For a recent comprehensive survey of the literature, see Kobayashi (2005a).

13. For an example conflating the two concepts, see Posner (2005), stating that "the usual purpose of bundling, as of tying, is price discrimination."

tion that has drawn the most attention from academics. The disproportion-ate attention to price discrimination is in part due to the path-dependent nature of the economics literature. While the economic analysis of bundling can be traced as far back as Augustin Cournot's 1897 proposal to address pric-ing externalities via complementary goods, the modern treatment of bundling is generally traced back to Stigler's analysis of block booking in the *Loew's* case.[14] While only indirectly related to the antitrust issues of interest today, the history of the academic literature subsequent to Stigler forcefully illustrates many of the defects in the academic discussion on bundling in general.

Stigler rejected the leverage theory used by the Supreme Court in *Loew's* and proposed an alternative explanation for the practice. Using an example, he showed that a multiproduct monopolist could increase profits by using block booking as a subtle form of price discrimination. In Stigler's example, there are two demanders, A and B, and two films, X and Y. The demands for the films are assumed to be negatively correlated, so A values film X more than B and film Y less than B. In the now familiar example, buyer A would pay $8,000 for film X and $2,500 for film Y. Buyer B would pay $7,000 for film X and $3,000 for film Y. If the films were priced separately, the monopolist would set the price of films X and Y at $7,000 and $2,500 respectively. He would sell two units of each film, and have revenues of $19,000. If, however, he engaged in pure bundling, he could sell a block that consisted of both films to both buyers for $10,000, and his revenues would rise to $20,000. Intuitively, when consumers' valuations are negatively cor-related, offering films in a block reduces the between-consumer variation in reservation values and allows the seller to extract more of the consumer sur-plus though a uniform block price.

Stigler presented some general evidence in support of his price discrimi-nation hypothesis.[15] However, Kenney and Klein's in-depth examination of the *Loew's* case found that the facts were not consistent with Stigler's price discrimination hypothesis.[16] Prices charged for the block were not uniform

14. See Cournot (1897); Stigler (1963), discussing *United States* v. *Loew's, Inc.,* 371 U.S. 38 (1962). Block booking refers to the sale of a bundle or package of films to television stations. In the *Loew's* case, the Supreme Court struck down the use of block sales based on a leverage theory. See also *United States* v. *Paramount Pictures, Inc.,* 344 U.S. 131 (1948).

15. See Stigler (1963, appendix A), showing that the share of receipts for individual movies varied widely from city to city and citing a study that suggested that the aggregate value of a television station could be reliably predicted from a few observable factors.

16. See Kenney and Klein (1983, 2000).

and varied across geographic markets. Moreover, in multiple-station markets, Loew's used competitive bidding to grant to a single station in a given geographic market the exclusive rights to broadcast the block of films. The use of competitive bidding would have provided an alternative way through which stations' reservation values for individual films could be revealed and thus would reduce Stigler's hypothesized reason for the use of the blocks in such markets.

This would not be the case in single-station markets, where competitive bidding would not be feasible. Thus a testable implication of the price discrimination theory would be that block booking would be more prevalent in single-station markets. Kenney and Klein instead found that the blocks were broken more frequently in the single-station markets than in markets where competitive bidding was used to price the block. Based on this finding, they reject the hypothesis that block booking was used to engage in third-degree price discrimination.

Kenney and Klein argue instead that the average pricing of a block of films was a way to minimize information costs associated with the sale of a standardized product. Block booking lowered information costs in two ways. First, it prevented television stations from investing in information with little private or social value. Second, block booking facilitated the accurate pricing of the standardized product by increasing the number of transactions and thus the quality of price information for the sales of a like product. Both effects would tend to reduce buyer search costs and increase the efficiency of the film distribution system.

Separate from its historical significance, the example of block booking illustrates the following lessons regarding the economic analysis of bundling. First, the example highlights the value of generating testable hypotheses and finding the data to carry out the tests. Whether or not the block booking of films was used as a price discrimination mechanism, price discrimination became the primary noncost-based explanation for bundling studied by economists. A large number of papers examined in depth the conditions under which a multiproduct monopolist could profitably use bundling to extract additional surplus.[17] However, if Kenney and Klein are correct, and price discrimination is an unlikely explanation for the practice in *Loew's*,

17. See, for example, Adams and Yellen (1976); Schmalensee (1984); McAfee, McMillian, and Whinston (1989); Salinger (1995).

then the absence of an early in-depth examination may have caused a type of path dependence in the economics literature that resulted in the intense study of a phenomenon of little empirical relevance.

Moreover, the focus on price discrimination may have diverted attention away from examining the real underlying reasons firms use bundling. Authors attempting to characterize the general conditions under which bundling facilitated rent extraction did not generally consider obvious bundling-specific efficiencies.[18] Furthermore, it may have delayed the search for less obvious reasons why bundling would be used. For example, Kenney and Klein's explanation for bundling-specific cost reductions does not flow from an observable reduction in "package costs." Rather, the efficiencies result from the alteration of incentive to engage in socially wasteful search, which would not be obvious in the absence of an in-depth examination of the institutions and markets involved.

Entry Deterrence and Exclusion

Of greater relevance to recent antitrust cases are the papers that examine the use of bundling as an exclusionary or entry-deterring device. For example, Nalebuff, in a series of papers, has demonstrated how bundling could be used by a monopolist in one market to reduce competition in a second market. In his entry deterrence model, a monopolist currently producing in two markets is faced with entry in one market.[19] Nalebuff demonstrates how pure bundling can reduce the residual demand facing a one-market entrant and thus reduce the profitability of entry. In some cases bundling deters entry that would have occurred in the absence of bundling. Moreover, Nalebuff shows that such entry deterrence can occur in the absence of a commitment to bundling, as the use of bundling can be optimal even when entry occurs.[20]

It is far from clear, however, what inferences can be drawn from Nalebuff's model and results. The standard criticisms of the theoretical literature apply to Nalebuff's model: it contains restrictive assumptions, including the

18. An exception is Salinger (1995, note 17).

19. Nalebuff (2004).

20. This feature distinguishes Nalebuff's result from that of Whinston (1990), which showed that tying could deter entry. In the latter's model a commitment to tying is required, as the monopolist would abandon tying if entry occurred.

assumption of monopoly, and does not address efficiencies arising from bundling. Even setting aside these standard criticisms, interpretation of the results is problematic because the article examines entry independent of the effect of bundling on welfare.[21] Moreover, if the welfare effects are considered, bundling generally increases welfare in the model. Relative to the no-bundling equilibrium with entry, welfare in almost any alternative equilibrium rises, including those equilibriums where bundling results in marginal entry deterrence.[22] Thus, based on a welfare standard, the model would imply that bundling, even if it deters entry, should not be condemned.

Critics of the welfare standard would argue that the model only considers short-run welfare and that the effect of entry deterrence would be felt over the long run. If so, then the models should be modified to consider such long-run or dynamic effects.[23] However, the ability to make general inferences or to formulate antitrust rules from models that explicitly consider dynamic or long-run effects is extremely limited.[24] Such models are either plagued by an inability to make specific predictions or require very restrictive assumptions to generate specific predictions. As a result, the power of such models is generally quite low.[25]

In related papers Nalebuff and Greenlee, Reitman, and Sibley demonstrate how bundling can be used as an exclusionary device.[26] In these models a monopolist in product Y engages in the bundling of Y and a competitively supplied good X. Absent bundling, the Y monopolist will set the price of Y equal to the stand-alone monopoly price m. Because the X market is assumed to be competitive, the price of X in the absence of bundling will equal the cost of production c.

Now consider a bundle that offers a small discount e on the price of Y for those consumers that agree to buy all of their units of X from the Y monopolist at a small premium d. This results in bundle prices for X and Y equal to $m - e$ and $c + d$, respectively. At the no-bundling monopoly price m, the

21. For a general criticism of this approach, see Demsetz (1982); von Weizsacker (1980).

22. Brennan (2005).

23. For an example of a model with dynamic or multiperiod effects, see Carlton and Waldman (2002).

24. Carlton and Waldman (2005) suggest that "a very cautions approach" to antitrust liability be taken based on such dynamic models.

25. See generally Kobayashi (1997).

26. Nalebuff (2005); Greenlee, Reitman, and Sibley (2004).

small decrease in the price of Y will have a second-order effect on profits. However, the small increase in the price of X will have a first-order effect on profits. Thus, for some small value of e and d, offering the bundle discount increases the profits of the monopolist. Moreover, for some small value of e and d, the bundle also will be preferred by consumers to the stand-alone prices m and c. Thus such bundle discounts increase both consumer welfare and total welfare. However, because the bundle is preferred to the stand-alone prices m and c, such a bundle discount can exclude an equally or even a more efficient competitor in the X market. Moreover, the Y monopolist does not have to price below cost in order to exclude competitors in the X market.

To illustrate these points, consider the following numerical example.[27] Let the demand for Y be given by $Q_Y = 100 - P_Y$, and let the demand for X be inelastic at 20. Y costs nothing to produce, and the marginal cost of producing X is 10. Equilibrium prices for X and Y absent bundling are 50 and 10, respectively. Now consider a bundle discount in which the price of Y is decreased to 49 for those who also purchase their X from the Y monopolist at a price of 11. By taking the lower price on Y, the consumer that buys the bundle saves at least 50 on the purchases of Y (one on each of fifty units of Y, plus the surplus from the fifty-first unit of Y). The consumer pays an additional 20 for the twenty units of X and thus is better off by at least 30. The monopolist's profits from the sale of Y fall by 1, from 2500 (50*50) to 2499 (49*51). However, the monopolist now makes an additional 20 on the sale of X. Thus both the monopolist and the consumer are better off with the bundle.

Although the bundle prices for both X and Y are above cost, equally efficient competitors in the X market will not sell any units when the bundle is offered. In order for stand-alone suppliers of X to make sales, they would have to offer the consumer savings of at least 30 (the consumer's net savings from the bundle). To generate savings of more than 30 on the sales of twenty units of X, the stand-alone price of X would have to be between 7 and 8, which would be below the cost of an equally efficient competitor and would also exclude a more efficient competitor with costs as low as 8.

In this example static consumer welfare and total welfare increase. In effect, because of the assumption that the demand for X is inelastic, the

---

27. This example is from Nalebuff (2005, note 26).

bundle implements a two-part tariff, which lowers the price of the good with the downward sloping demand curve, thus reducing the deadweight losses from monopoly.[28] Because this bundle discount would exclude a hypothetically equally efficient competitor, Nalebuff—and those who would adopt this standard—would condemn such bundled discounts based on their exclusionary effect.[29] As was the case with Nalebuff's entry deterrence result, use of such a test would erroneously condemn welfare-increasing conduct.[30]

However, not all forms of bundled discounts increase consumer or total surplus. Both Nalebuff and Greenlee and others consider a bundled discount where the bundle is priced at $m + c$, but the stand-alone price for the monopoly good is increased above m.[31] Once again, consumers prefer the bundle to the stand-alone prices so that an equally efficient competitor would be excluded, being unable to make sales at c. Moreover, in this case consumer welfare unambiguously falls. Consumers that purchase the bundle are indifferent, as the bundle prices are equal to the nonbundled stand-alone prices. The same is true for those who purchase X at the stand-alone price c. But consumers that purchase Y at the stand-alone price are made worse off. Thus consumer surplus must fall under these circumstances.

Because an equally efficient competitor would be excluded, this bundle offer would fail Nalebuff's equally efficient competitor test. Because consumer welfare falls, Greenlee, Reitman, and Sibley would also condemn such bundle offers on antitrust grounds. This leads the latter group to propose the following test for welfare-decreasing bundled discounts. Under the assumption that the bundle prices are optimal, a bundle discount will decrease consumer surplus if the stand-alone price for good Y is above the monopoly price of Y in the absence of bundling. Such welfare-reducing bundle discounts would be found to violate the antitrust laws. This kind of test is more conservative than the equally efficient competitor test suggested by Nalebuff. It would leave alone those bundled discounts that actually

28. In effect, the overcharge on X serves as the entry fee. See generally Oi (1971).

29. The exclusion result does not follow if the monopolist can source production of X from competitive suppliers. The monopolist is indifferent between producing X himself and purchasing X from an equally efficient competitive supplier at 10. Indeed, if the competitive suppliers are more efficient, the monopolist would be better off purchasing these units at a price below 10 and reselling them in the bundle at 11. See Schmalensee (1982).

30. See Nalebuff (2004, note 19 and accompanying text).

31. Nalebuff (2005); Greenlee, Reitman, and Sibley (2004).

yielded lower prices to consumers and only condemn those where the bundle discount is only a discount compared to inflated stand-alone prices.

On the other hand, such a test may be difficult to implement. Accepting for the moment the validity of the model, carrying out the test suggested by Greenlee and others would require a comparison between the existing stand-alone price for the monopoly good Y offered in conjunction with the bundle with the optimal monopoly price that would be charged in the absence of bundling. While this task is well defined within the context of a theoretical model with known and stable demand, such an undertaking is likely to be much more difficult to implement in practice.[32]

Taken as a whole, the literature on exclusionary bundling provides the following useful results. First, bundled discounts can exclude or deter the entry of equally efficient competitors. Second, this exclusion can occur at prices that are above cost. Third, bundled discounts that exclude equally efficient competitors can increase or decrease consumer and total welfare.

On the other hand, the literature, as it currently stands, does not go beyond showing that such effects are possible. Because of the lack of empirical work, there is little or no evidence that such harm is likely under real world conditions. The models contain many restrictive assumptions. The models assume that the firm selling Y has an actual monopoly. In practice, firms rarely have a market share equal to 1, and little attention has been paid to considering how the existence of competition in the market for Y might affect their results. This latter point is important given that under the antitrust laws, firms that face some competition in all markets can be found to possess *market power*, which is often erroneously equated with *monopoly power*.[33]

Moreover, both the Nalebuff and Greenlee papers ignore the large and varied reasons why bundling might be used. For example, neither paper considers alternative explanations for bundling based on inducing self-selection by heterogeneous consumers.[34] Nor do these models consider how

---

32. The test would require the estimation of the but-for-bundling optimal price of Y. One proxy for this would be the direct observation of the price of good Y before the monopolist began bundling. However, such prices are not always available, and changes in demand and cost conditions may make such a proxy unreliable. In such cases estimating the but-for-monopoly price would require an econometric estimation that controlled for these changing variables.

33. See, for example, Klein (1993).

34. Consideration of such issues would further complicate application of the test created by Green-

their results would be affected by efficiencies from bundling. Moreover, while they analogize the use of bundled rebates to tying and exclusive dealing, they do not consider the procompetitive reasons why manufacturers adopt such policies. And while others have studied these procompetitive uses in the context of exclusive dealing and tying, this work has not been undertaken in the context of bundling and bundled rebates. As a result these models do not provide a reliable way to gauge whether the potential for harm would outweigh any demonstrable benefits from the practice.

Antitrust and Bundling

The importance of better understanding why bundling occurs and how bundling affects markets has been highlighted by recent developments in the antitrust laws. The first part of this section briefly reviews the Third Circuit Court's recent decision in *LePage's* v. *3M* and its implications for bundling. The second part evaluates some of the tests for anticompetitive bundling that have been suggested in the economics literature.

Bundling and Antitrust Law: LePage's v. 3M

In *LePage's* v. *3M*, the Third Circuit Court of Appeals upheld a jury verdict that found 3M's use of bundled rebates violated section 2 of the Sherman Antitrust Act.[35] 3M's bundled rebates gave large retailers (such as Wal-Mart, K-Mart, and Target) discounts if they purchased certain volumes of various 3M products. The size of the bundled rebates increased when retailers met volume goals across six product categories, with the largest rebates being given to retailers that met the volume targets in all six categories. The use of bundled rebates was challenged by LePage's, the leading manufacturer of unbranded transparent tape. LePage's alleged that 3M's use of bundled rebates caused retailers to drop LePage's as a supplier not

---

lee, Reitman, and Sibley, as the stand-alone prices for *X* and *Y* associated with mixed bundling are often higher than the optimal prices for *X* and *Y* in the absence of bundling. See Adams and Yellen (1976, note 17) for an example of mixed bundling with these characteristics. See also Kolay and Shaffer (2003).

35. *LePage's, Inc.* v. *3M*, 324 F.3d 141 (3d Cir. 2003). For a detailed discussion of the case, see Rubinfeld (2005).

because of competition on the merits but rather because of the possibility that they might fail to qualify for the largest rebates. A jury found that 3M's practices violated section 2 of the Sherman Act. A Third Circuit panel reversed this verdict.[36] However, the Third Circuit, sitting en banc, upheld the jury's verdict on the bundling claims.

Despite noting that the Third Circuit's en banc decision rested on an incomplete record and a poorly articulated theory of economic harm, the United States, in its brief to the Supreme Court in *3M* v. *LePage's*, urged the Court not to take the case.[37] While the government recognized that "the business community and consumers would benefit from clear, objective guidance on the application of the Section 2 to bundled rebates," it had little confidence that this case would provide the Court "a suitable vehicle" for providing such guidance. In addition to the identified shortcomings of the case record and decision, the government's position was influenced by the judiciary's relative lack of experience with this issue and the underdeveloped nature of the "relatively recent and sparse" academic literature on bundling.[38]

The Supreme Court declined to review the case.[39] By deferring consideration of the issues presented in *3M* v. *LePage's*, the Court chose to await a case with a record better adapted to development of an appropriate stan-

---

36. *LePage's, Inc.* v. *3M*, 277 F.3d 365 (3d Cir. 2002).

37. See *Brief of the United States as Amicus Curiae*, 2004 WL 120591 (May 28, 2004), p. 16, noting that the Third Circuit "failed to explain precisely why the evidence supported a jury verdict of liability in this case, including what precisely rendered 3M's conduct unlawful."

38. Before *LePage's* there was only one reported decision in the federal courts that condemned the use of bundled rebates on antitrust grounds. See *SmithKline Corp.* v. *Eli Lilly and Co.*, 575 F.2d 1056 (3d Cir. 1978). In the only other case involving an antitrust challenge to the use of bundled rebates, the defendant prevailed on summary judgment. See *Ortho Diagnostic Systems, Inc.* v. *Abbot Labs., Inc.*, 920 F. Supp. 455, 471 (S.D.N.Y. 1996). Other cases involving loyalty or volume discounts that spanned multiple markets or submarkets include *Advo, Inc.* v. *Philadelphia Newspapers, Inc.*, 51 F.3d 1191 (3d Cir. 1995), affirming summary judgment for the defendant under the *Matsushita* predatory pricing test (*Matsushita Electrical Industries Co.* v. *Zenith Radio Corp.*, 475 U.S. 574 [1986]); and *Virgin Atlantic Airways, Ltd.* v. *British Airways, Plc.*, 257 F.3d 256 (2d Cir. 2000), affirming summary judgment for the defendant under the *Brooke Group* test (see discussion of this test in the latter half of this chapter). In both these cases, the defendant prevailed on summary judgment.

Internationally, the European Union has condemned a large number of pricing policies by dominant firms, including the policies used by British Airways that were the subject of the aforementioned U.S. case. See *British Airways* v. *Commission*, Case T-219/99, 2003 ECR II-5917 (2003). The European Union has also condemned the use of bundled rebates by tire maker Michelin. See *Michelin* v. *Commission*, Case T-203/01, 2003 ECR II-4071 (2003). For a summary see Cooper and others (2005).

39. *3M* v. *LePage's*, 124 S. Ct. 2932 (2004), certiorari denied.

dard and, as urged by the United States in its brief, could allow "the case law and economic analysis to develop further." In principle, the cautious approach urged by the United States in its brief and implicitly chosen by the Court is understandable. In general, the federal courts have taken a cautious approach to the expansion of antitrust liability under section 2 of the Sherman Act. Even in cases where the economic literature on vertical practices is relatively developed, it is not so easy for the courts in real world situations to distinguish between pro- and anticompetitive vertical restrictions. And without a reliable way to distinguish pro- and anticompetitive uses, any rule that condemned such a ubiquitous practice without a showing of likely harm to competition would result in the widespread condemnation of efficient practices.[40] Such a result would be particularly damaging to the economy as it would chill the very conduct the antitrust laws are designed to protect.[41]

Given the ubiquity of bundling, the courts' lack of experience with it, and the paucity of empirical evidence regarding the relative prevalence of exclusionary versus procompetitive uses of bundling and bundled rebates, these arguments for a cautious approach would seem to apply a fortiori to the application of section 2 to bundling. Although the United States and the Supreme Court exercised such caution, the Third Circuit, in its en banc opinion in *LePage's*, failed to do so. The Third Circuit concluded that it was sufficient for LePage's to prove that it could not compete with 3M's bundled rebates because "they may foreclose portions of the market to a potential competitor who does not manufacture an equally diverse group of products and who therefore cannot make a comparable offer."[42] Although the Third Circuit suggested that 3M's bundled rebates could exclude an equally efficient competitor, it did not cite any evidence that an equally efficient competitor would have been excluded by 3M's bundled rebates. Thus the Third Circuit would allow a jury to find a dominant firm liable under the antitrust laws based on the *possibility* that bundled rebates, including those that *increase* consumer welfare, could exclude an equally efficient competitor that produces a less diverse set of products.[43] The plaintiff would not

---

40. Courts and commentators have generally recognized the potential costs of antitrust enforcement under section 2 of the Sherman Act that would condemn a ubiquitously used vertical practice. See, for example, Evans and Padilla (2005, note 7).

41. See *United States* v. *Microsoft*, 253 F.3d 34, 69 (D.C. Cir. 2001); *Verizon Communications, Inc.* v. *Law Offices of Curtis V. Trinko, LLP,* 124 S. Ct. 872, 882 (2004).

42. *LePage's, Inc.* v. *3M*, 324 F.3d 141, 177 (3d Cir. 2003), note 35.

43. Other courts have considered antitrust harm based on similar theoretical arguments but have

have to show that it was an equally efficient competitor, nor would it have to prove that the bundled rebates in question would have, in fact, excluded a hypothetical equally efficient competitor.

As a result the *LePage's* case has generated much uncertainty over the legality of a ubiquitous practice. The Third Circuit exposed to potential antitrust liability any firm found to possess sufficient market power that chooses to offer discounts on a bundle that contains products that are also sold separately by businesses that sell only a subset of these products. The potential for liability could deter such firms from offering a bundle that would reduce prices for consumers and provide higher consumer welfare. Thus this decision is likely to impose the high type I error costs (costs associated with erroneously condemning or deterring an efficient business practice) the federal courts have been so careful to avoid in the past.

Moreover, the effect of *LePage's* has not been limited to the Third Circuit or to bundled rebates. For example, in *McKenzie-Willamette Hospital* v. *PeaceHealth*, the plaintiff McKenzie, who operated a hospital that offered primary health services, successfully argued that a contract between Peace-Health, a firm that operated hospitals that provided a more expansive range of services, and two preferred provider organizations contained an unlawful bundled discount.[44] In a stark example of the type of result made possible by the Third Circuit's standard-free ruling in *LePage's*, the court instructed the jury that "bundled pricing occurs when price discounts are offered for purchasing an entire line of services exclusively from one supplier. Bundled price discounts may be anticompetitive if they are offered by a monopolist and substantially foreclose portions of the market to a competitor who does not provide an equally diverse group of services and who therefore cannot make a comparable offer."

---

rejected them when not supported by any evidence. See, for example, *Virgin Atlantic,* p. 270–1, note 38 (rejecting theory because of a lack of evidence); *Ortho,* p. 471, note 38 ("a party may not rest on economic theories that may or may not apply to the facts of the case or on conclusory or incomplete expert analyses any more than it may rest on unsubstantiated allegations of its pleadings"); and *Advo,* pp. 1198–99, note 38.

44. *McKenzie-Willamette Hospital* v. *PeaceHealth,* Case No. 02-6032-HA, 2004 WL 3168282 (D. Or., 2004) (denial of renewed motion for directed verdict).

Figure 2-1. *Tests for Anticompetitive Conduct*

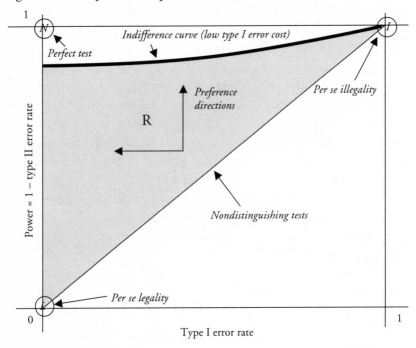

Evaluating Anticompetitive Tests

Beyond criticizing the *LePage's* decision for its standard-free approach to the problem, the issue to be addressed is how to come up with a standard that can be applied to the use of bundling by dominant firms. In general, the optimal standard would be one that minimized the sum of direct costs and error costs.[45] Error costs include the costs of type I errors and the costs of type II errors (the costs of allowing anticompetitive conduct).[46] Direct costs include those associated with the administration of, compliance with, and litigation over the antitrust laws.

The choice of an optimal test will depend on the cost and frequency of the relative types of errors, and on the costs of administration. Figure 2-1 illustrates the trade-off between type I and type II errors. The horizontal axis shows a test's rate of type I error. The vertical axis shows the power of a test, equal to 1 minus the test's rate of type II error. From an error cost standpoint, an ideal test would be at point *N*, where both the type I and type II

45. See generally Posner (2002); Evans and Padilla (2005, note 7).

error rates equal zero. However, such a point is generally not attainable or only attainable at a prohibitive cost. Certainly, in the case of applying section 2 to bundling by dominant firms, any test will be far from perfect. The forty-five-degree line indicates tests where the probability of finding anti-competitive behavior is the same whether or not the underlying behavior was anticompetitive or not. The standard-free approach in the *LePage's* case would lie somewhere on this line.

Moreover, rules of per se legality and per se illegality are on this line. Per se rules are simple bright-line tests that simply focus on determining whether or not certain conduct took place. Point *I* represents a rule of per se illegality, which would condemn all conduct covered by the rule. Point *L* represents a rule of per se legality; conduct covered by this rule would be immune from the antitrust laws. While such per se rules are not useful for the purposes of distinguishing anti- and procompetitive conduct, they may be useful as bright-line administrative rules. A rule of per se illegality would be rational if the conduct in question involved behavior that was almost certain to be socially undesirable and if such conduct could be reliably distinguished from other types of behavior. While in general it is optimal to trade off type I and type II errors, such a trade-off is not necessary in such cases because the danger of condemning socially desirable behavior is minimal. Naked horizontal price fixing is often argued to have these attributes.[47]

These conditions are illustrated in figure 2-1, which contains a social indifference curve that reflects the trade-off between the expected cost of type I and type II errors. In general, the shape of these social indifference curves will depend on the magnitude of the cost and relative frequency of each type of error.[48] Under the assumption that naked horizontal price fixing involves activity that is almost certain to be socially undesirable, the frequency and thus the total expected cost of type I errors is close to zero. Under these circumstances the social indifference curves will be near horizontal and a rule of per se illegality will result in total error costs that are nearly identical to the total error costs associated with using an ideal test at point *N*. Both tests correctly condemn anticompetitive behavior. And the expected costs of type

46. See generally Easterbrook (1984), discussing relative magnitudes of type I and type II errors in antitrust cases.

47. But see Kobayashi (2001), discussing the characterization issue.

48. See generally Cooper and others (2005, note 38), explaining how differences in U.S. and European Union enforcement result from differing evaluations of the relative costs of type I and type II errors.

Figure 2-2. *Tests for Anticompetitive Bundling and the Feasible Set*[a]

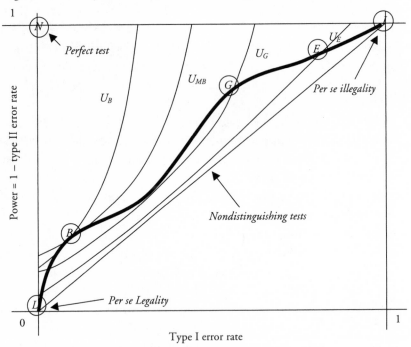

a. See text for explanation of lettered lines and points.

I error are similar for both tests even though the rate of type I error for test *N* is zero, while the rate of type I error for test *I* is one. This is because the near-zero frequency of procompetitive naked horizontal price fixing keeps the expected costs of committing type I errors under test *I* low. With such preference curves, a rule of per se illegality would dominate any equal cost test in the shaded area **R** in figure 2-1. Moreover, per se tests are likely to have lower direct costs than tests that actually attempt to distinguish pro- and anticompetitive behavior.

Figure 2-2 depicts other tests that have been considered by the courts or proposed by academics. Point *B* depicts the application of the *Brooke Group* test to bundled rebates. The *Brooke Group* case involved a challenge to the use of volume discounts on generic cigarettes.[49] The Supreme Court upheld the dismissal of a $148.8 million jury award. The Court held that plaintiffs who allege predatory pricing under section 2 of the Sherman Act or under

49. *Brooke Group* v. *Brown and Williamson Tobacco Corp.*, 509 U.S. 209 (1993).

the Robinson-Patman Act must satisfy two "not easy to establish" requirements. First, the plaintiff must prove that the alleged predatory prices are
"below an appropriate measure" of the defendant's costs.[50] Second, the plaintiff must demonstrate that the defendant had a reasonable prospect—or
under section 2, a dangerous probability—of recouping its investment in
below-cost prices.[51]

In addressing the potential for error costs of using such a standard, the
Court noted that any exclusionary effect from above-cost prices either
"reflects the lower cost structure of the alleged predator, and so represents
competition on the merits, or is beyond the practical ability of a judicial tri-
bunal to control without courting intolerable risks of chilling legitimate
price cutting." Stated in terms of the error costs, the Supreme Court set out
a test for predatory pricing that minimized the probability of a type I error
while tolerating a higher cost of type II error. This kind of test would lie in
the lower left error cost space of figure 2-2.

Such a choice would be rational if the expected costs of type II errors are
small relative to the expected costs of type I errors. The Court noted that successful predation, while theoretically possible, is rare.[52] Thus, in contrast to
the social indifference curve depicted in figure 2-1, the social indifference
curves for predation are likely to have a steep slope. Under these conditions
a rule that has the error characteristics of the *Brooke Group* rule will dominate any test that lies below and to the right of the indifference curve labeled
U_B in figure 2.

However, it may be the case that the trade-offs involved in the single-price
predation case are different from those that apply to the case of bundled
rebates. As discussed earlier, there are theoretical models that show that
bundling can allow a monopolist to engage in above-cost exclusion. In such
cases the second prong of the *Brooke Group* test, the ability to recoup losses,
is not an issue. Accordingly, the trade-offs between type I and type II errors
that are applicable to the single-product case of price predation may differ
from those that apply to bundled discounts.[53]

50. In *Brooke Group*, the parties agreed that the appropriate measure of costs was average variable
costs. See *Brooke Group*, p. 222, note 49.
51. *Brooke Group*, p. 224, note 49.
52. *Brooke Group*, pp. 220–24, note 49. See also Easterbrook (1981); Lott (1999); McGee (1958,
1980). For a theoretical example of successful predation, see the model of Milgrom and Roberts (1982),
showing that predation is possible if there is a small probability that the predator is irrational.
53. See Kobayashi (2005b), noting a similar distinction made by some U.S. federal courts.

The possibility that above-cost exclusion is possible does not mean that the *Brooke Group* rule, modified for the case of bundled discounts, is no longer optimal.[54] First, it is not clear that the relevant indifference curves in the case of a rule applying section 2 to bundled discounts will differ much from those applicable to the single-product price predation case. Even if one accepts that the potential for type II errors may have increased in the case of bundled discounts, the existence of demonstrable and ubiquitous benefits from bundling suggests that any antitrust rule applying section 2 to a bundled discount would also be associated with an increase in the cost of type I errors. Thus, ex ante, it is unclear which way the trade-off would shift.

Second, even if an increased potential for anticompetitive harm flattens out the indifference curves (in figure 2-2, from U_B to U_{MB}), the modified *Brooke Group* (*MB*) rule may still be preferred to any feasible alternative test.[55] As depicted in figure 2-2, test *B* would still dominate alternative tests shown at points *G* and point *E*. (These tests are described below.) Whether or not this is actually the case will depend on what alternatives are available. Consider the equally efficient competitor test suggested by Nalebuff and others.[56] As Greenlee, Reitman, and Sibley note, such a test is overinclusive and does not distinguish between offending bundle discounts that raise or lower consumer welfare.[57] A test with these characteristics would arguably lie near the forty-five-degree line in the upper right corner of the error cost space. Test *E* depicts such a test. Unless the social indifference curves were flat, reflecting a low expected cost of type I errors, such a test, located in the upper right portion of the error cost space, is unlikely to be optimal.

One way to generate flatter social indifference curves would be to limit the application of test *E* to situations where the costs of type I error are diminished.[58] For example, the influential Areeda and Hovenkamp treatise suggests a test that would condemn use of bundled rebates by firms with

54. One such rule would require a plaintiff to prove that the price of the bundle is above the appropriate measure of the cost of the bundle. A second variant, discussed later, would attempt to allocate the bundle discount among its components.

55. See Timothy J. Muris, "Antitrust Law, Economics, and Bundled Discounts," submitted on behalf of the United States Telecom Association in response to the Antitrust Modernization Commission's request for public comments, July 15, 2005 (www.amc.gov/public_studies_fr28902/exclus_conduct_pdf/050715_US_Telecom-Exclus_Conduct-Bundling.pdf).

56. Nalebuff (2005).

57. Greenlee, Reitman, and Sibley (2004).

58. For a discussion of this issue in the context of criminal antitrust enforcement, see Kobayashi (2001, note 47).

monopoly power if a hypothetical equally efficient competitor would be excluded. However, the treatise would limit its application to situations of near monopoly, suggesting that

> in any event, the theory should not be extended to situations involving substantially smaller market shares or significant uncertainty about market definition. The defendant in this case [*LePage's*] was conceded to be the dominant firm with a historic market share of 90 percent in what appeared to be a well-defined market. Indeed, unless there is evidence of collusive behavior, we would be reluctant to extend the doctrine to any situation in which there was at least one competing firm able to match the defendant's discount across all product lines."[59]

In all other cases, bundled discounts would be treated under the treatise's approach to package pricing, which would not condemn package discounts as long as the price of the package exceeds the total cost of the package.

To the extent that these limits are followed, such an approach will limit the costs of type I error by confining application of the hypothetical equally efficient competitor test to situations where the perceived threat is the greatest.[60] A modified version of the *Brooke Group* test could be applied elsewhere. However, it is far from clear that antitrust plaintiffs, courts, and juries will adhere to such limits. While the possession of monopoly power is one of the two necessary elements of a section 2 case, many courts use the term *market power* and *monopoly power* interchangeably. Market power, possessed by a large number of firms in a wide variety of markets, is a much broader concept than monopoly power.[61] Even if the equally efficient competitor test was limited to firms with "substantial market power," such a term is likely

---

59. Areeda and Hovenkamp (2005, p. 184, para. 749).

60. As noted above, there is little or no evidence to suggest that the potential threat from exclusionary bundling by dominant firms would outweigh any efficiencies such firms gain from bundling. Note that firms that fail the liability test could in theory escape liability by bearing the burden of proving that they had a legitimate business justification for the practice. However, meeting this burden is not so easy in practice. See Epstein (2005). The procompetitive reasons firms engage in bundling can be complex, have largely been ignored in the economic literature, and as a result are not well understood. Thus communicating these reasons to a judge or jury may be difficult.

61. Klein (1993, note 33).

to expand well beyond firms with near monopoly or with market shares in well-defined markets greater than 90 percent.[62]

Another potential alternative would be the test suggested by Greenlee, Reitman, and Sibley.[63] As noted earlier, this test would only condemn instances of exclusionary bundling that resulted in consumer welfare falling. In contrast, the hypothetical equally efficient competitor test would not make any such distinction. Relative to test E, this test (labeled test G in figure 2-2) would have a lower rate of type I error. Thus test G would lie to the left of test E.

Given that test G differentiates between welfare-decreasing and welfare-increasing bundled discounts, and only condemns the former, a perfectly administered test G should coincide with the ideal test (test N). However, this is not likely to be the case for two primary reasons. As discussed earlier, the Greenlee test requires knowledge or estimation of the but-for monopoly price and likely will be difficult to administer in many cases. As a result such a test will be relatively more costly to administer, and it also likely will be administered with error. As the First Circuit noted in *Barry Wright* v. *ITT Grinnell Co.*: "Unlike economics, law is an administrative system, the effects of which depend upon the content of rules and precedents only as they are applied by judges and juries in courts and by lawyers advising their clients. Rules that seek to embody every economic complexity and qualification may well, through the vagaries of administration, prove counterproductive, undercutting the very economic end they seek to serve."[64]

Therefore, tests that are complex and difficult to administer will fall far short of the ideal test at point N. Indeed, because of the potential for errors in administration of the test, it is possible that the rate of type II error under test G will be greater than under test E. More generally, these effects cause complex and hard to administer tests to lie closer to the forty-five-degree line than to the ideal test at point N.[65] A similar effect will result from use of tests derived from models that are based on critical assumptions that do not hold in practice. A test that works well given the strict assumptions of a theoret-

---

62. See Elhauge (2003), citing examples and suggesting a threshold of 50 percent.

63. Greenlee, Reitman, and Sibley (2004).

64. 724 F.2d 227, 234 (1st Cir. 1983).

65. If the test was so complex and burdensome to administer, it would be possible, in theory, for the test to lie below the forty-five-degree line. Such a test would give perverse results—that is, welfare-increasing conduct would be condemned with higher probability than welfare-decreasing conduct.

ical model may perform poorly when confronted with real markets. Again, the effect is to move tests that are close to test N in theory, but not in practice, toward the forty-five-degree line. Such a result is more likely when the models and their assumptions have not been checked for robustness or tested empirically.

Because of the relatively underdeveloped nature of the economic literature, it is likely that any new tests, based on the current economic understanding of bundling, will suffer the same fate and lie closer to the forty-five-degree line than to the ideal test at point N. Figure 2-2 illustrates the likely feasible set of current and future tests given the current state of knowledge.[66] Given the indifference curves shown in figure 2-2, the feasible set would have to expand significantly away from the forty-five-degree line toward point N in order for any test to improve on the error cost trade-off of test B. The fact that the feasible set consists of tests that do not lie far from the forty-five-degree line makes it more likely that tests that lie near one of the per se corner solutions will be optimal.

The discussion so far has not addressed the issue of direct costs. The relative rankings illustrated by the isopreference curves depicted in the figures are for tests that have equal direct costs. However, some tests will result in higher direct costs than others. As noted above, an advantage of both of the per se tests is that the costs of administering such them will be relatively low. In addition, low administrative costs have also been suggested as reasons in favor of using both test E and test B.[67] Moreover, to the extent that these tests will result in lower direct costs than test G, test B will be preferred to test G even if both lie on the same indifference curve. As depicted in figure 2-2, this consideration will make the case for test B over test G stronger.

The cost and administrability issues are also relevant to the question of how one would modify the *Brooke Group* test in the case of bundled discounts. As noted above, a simple approach would be to compare the price of the bundle, with discount, to the appropriate cost of the bundle. Some have criticized such a rule as too permissive and suggest that the bundle discount be allocated among the component goods. The problem with such an approach is that there is no consensus, in theory or in practice, on how to

---

66. As depicted in figure 2-2, the feasible set is the area between the forty-five-degree line and the curve through the points *LBGEI*.

67. Areeda and Hovenkamp (2005, p. 182, note 59).

make such allocations. The problem will often require a court to allocate joint and common costs among the products in the bundle.[68] Unless this is done in an arbitrary fashion (for example, through a pro rata rule), such a task is likely to be an administrative nightmare for the courts. And an arbitrary decision can simultaneously increase both types of error costs.[69]

Conclusion

The economic literature on bundling has made many theoretical advances. However, several omissions reveal themselves. The advances have largely been on the theoretical side. These models contain restrictive assumptions regarding the existence of monopoly in some markets and the nature of rivalry in others. The models generally ignore obvious and ubiquitous reasons firms may use bundled discounts. These models have not been subject to robustness checks nor have their assumptions been tested empirically. As a result the literature that shows the possibility of anticompetitive harm does not provide a reliable way to gauge whether the potential for harm would outweigh any demonstrable benefits from the practice.

As a result of the underdeveloped nature of the literature, simple rules that result in extreme trade-offs between type I and type II errors may dominate more complex tests that attempt to differentiate procompetitive from anticompetitive behavior. Such complex tests may work well within the confines of a theoretical model but not when applied to firms in actual antitrust cases. Improving the reliability of more complex tests for anticompetitive behavior will require economists to expand their understanding of both the anticompetitive and procompetitive reasons firms engage in bundling. This will entail studying the reasons bundling is adopted by firms without market power, relaxing the assumption of monopoly in theoretical models, and generating testable hypotheses and the data to test them.

68. For an example of this issue, see *Virgin Atlantic*, pp. 267–69, note 38.

69. One suggested variant of the *Brooke Group* rule would be to allocate the entire bundle discount to the product or products produced by the plaintiff's firm. Such a rule would be equivalent to test *E* and thus would significantly increase the rate of type I error. Some have suggested that such a rule be used as a safe harbor. But there is little consensus on how one would proceed when the safe harbor test is not met. Nor is it clear how one could prevent the safe harbor from becoming the de facto substantive test that separates legal from illegal bundling.

References

Adams, William J., and Janet L. Yellen. 1976. "Commodity Bundling and the Burden of Monopoly." *Quarterly Journal of Economics* 90, no. 3: 475–98.

Areeda, Phillip E., and Herbert Hovenkamp. 2005. *Antitrust Law: An Analysis of Antitrust Principles and Their Application*, vol. 3 (2005 suppl.). New York: Aspen.

Brennan, Timothy J. 2005. "Competition as an Entry Barrier? Consumer and Total Welfare Benefits of Bundling." Related Publication 5-08. AEI-Brookings Joint Center for Regulatory Studies.

Carlton, Dennis W., and Michael Waldman. 2002. "The Strategic Use of Tying to Preserve and Create Market Power in Evolving Industries." *RAND Journal of Economics* 33, no. 2: 194–220.

———. 2005. "How Economics Can Improve Antitrust Doctrine towards Tie-In Sales." *Competition Policy International* 1, no. 1: 27–40.

Cooper, James C., and others. 2005. "A Comparative Study of United States and European Union Approaches to Vertical Policy." Working Paper 05-11. Vanderbilt University.

Cournot, Augustin. 1897. *Research into the Mathematical Principles of the Theory of Wealth*. Translated by Nathaniel T. Bacon. New York: Macmillan.

Demsetz, Harold. 1982. "Barriers to Entry." *American Economic Review* 72, no. 1: 47–57.

Easterbrook, Frank. 1981. "Predatory Strategies and Counterstrategies." *University of Chicago Law Review* 48, no. 2: 263–337.

———. 1984. "The Limits of Antitrust." *Texas Law Review* 63 (August): 1–40.

Elhauge, Einer. 2003. "Defining Better Monopolization Standards." *Stanford Law Review* 53 (November): 253–344.

Epstein, Richard A. 2005. "Monopoly Dominance or Level Playing Field: The New Antitrust Paradox." *University of Chicago Law Review* 72 (Winter): 49–72.

Evans, David S., and A. Jorge Padilla. 2005. "Designing Antitrust Rules for Assessing Unilateral Practices: A Neo-Chicago Approach." *University of Chicago Law Review* 72 (Winter): 73–98.

Evans, David S., and Michael Salinger. 2005. "Why Do Firms Bundle and Tie? Evidence from Competitive Markets and Implications for Tying Law." *Yale Journal on Regulation* 22, no. 1: 37–89.

Gavil, Andrew. 2004. "Exclusionary Distribution Strategies by Dominant Firms: Striking a Better Balance." *Antitrust Law Journal* 72, no. 1: 3–81.

Greenlee, Patrick, David Reitman, and David Sibley. 2004. "An Antitrust Analysis of Bundled Loyalty Discounts." Mimeo. U.S. Department of Justice, Antitrust Division.

Heide, Jan B., Shantanu Dutta, and Mark Bergen. 1998. "Exclusive Dealing and Business Efficiency: Evidence from Industry Practice." *Journal of Law and Economics* 41, no. 2: 387–407.

Kenney, Roy, and Benjamin Klein. 1983. "The Economics of Block Booking." *Journal of Law and Economics* 26, no. 3: 497–540.

———. 2000. "How Block Booking Facilitated Self-Enforcing Film Contracts." *Journal of Law and Economics* 43, no. 2: 427–35.

Klein, Benjamin. 1993. "Market Power in Antitrust: Economic Analysis after *Kodak*." *Supreme Court Economic Review* 3: 43–92.

———. 2003. "Exclusive Dealing as Competition for Distribution 'on the Merits.'" *George Mason Law Review* 12 (Fall): 119–62.

Klein, Benjamin, and Joshua Wright. 2005. "The Economics of Slotting Arrangements." Mimeo. George Mason University.

Kobayashi, Bruce H. 1997. "Game Theory and Antitrust: A Post-Mortem." *George Mason Law Review* 5 (Spring): 411–21.

———. 2001. "Antitrust, Agency, and Amnesty: An Economic Analysis of the Criminal Enforcement of the Antitrust Laws against Corporations." *George Washington Law Review* 56 (October-December): 715–44.

———. 2005a. "Does Economics Provide a Reliable Guide to Regulating Commodity Bundling by Firms? A Survey of the Economic Literature." *Journal of Competition Law and Economics* 1, no. 4: 707–46.

———. 2005b. "The Economics of Loyalty Discounts and Antitrust Law in the United States." *Competition Policy International* 1, no. 2: 115–48.

Kolay, Sreya, and Greg Shaffer. 2003. "Bundling and Menus of Two-Part Tariffs." *Journal of Industrial Economics* 51, no. 3: 383–403.

Lott, John R., Jr. 1999. *Are Predatory Commitments Credible? Who Should the Courts Believe?* University of Chicago Press.

Marvel, Howard. 1982. "Exclusive Dealing." *Journal of Law and Economics* 25, no. 1: 1–25.

McAfee, R. Preston, John McMillian, and Michael D. Whinston. 1989. "Multiproduct Monopoly, Commodity Bundling, and Correlation of Values." *Quarterly Journal of Economics* 104, no. 2: 371–83.

McGee, John S. 1958. "Predatory Price Cutting: The Standard Oil (N.J.) Case." *Journal of Law and Economics* 1 (April): 137–69.

———. 1980. "Predatory Pricing Revisited." *Journal of Law and Economics* 23, no. 2: 289–330.

Milgrom, Paul, and John Roberts. 1982. "Predation, Reputation, and Entry Deterrence." *Journal of Economic Theory* 27, no. 2: 280–312.

Mills, David E. 2004. "Market Share Discounts." Mimeo. University of Virginia.

Nalebuff, Barry. 2004. "Bundling as an Entry Barrier." *Quarterly Journal of Economics* 119, no. 1: 159–87.

———. 2005. "Exclusionary Bundling." Mimeo. Yale University.

Oi, Walter Y. 1971."A Disneyland Dilemma: Two-Part Tariffs for a Mickey Mouse Monopoly." *Quarterly Journal of Economics* 85 (February): 77–96.

Posner, Richard A. 2002. *Economic Analysis of Law.* 6th ed. New York: Aspen.

———. 2005. "Vertical Restraints and Antitrust Policy." *University of Chicago Law Review* 72 (Winter): 229–41.

Rubinfeld, Daniel L. 2005. "3M's Bundled Rebates: An Economic Perspective." *University of Chicago Law Review* 72 (Winter): 243–64.

Salinger, Michael A. 1995. "A Graphical Analysis of Bundling." *Journal of Business* 68 (January): 85–98.

Schmalensee, Richard. 1982. "Commodity Bundling by Single-Product Monopolies." *Journal of Law and Economics* 25 (April): 67–71.

———. 1984. "Gaussian Demand and Commodity Bundling." *Journal of Business* 57 (January): S211–30.

Stigler, George J. 1963. "*U.S.* v. *Loew's Inc.*: A Note on Block Booking." *Supreme Court Review 1963.* 152–57.

Telser, Lester G. 1972. "Advertising and Competition." *Journal of Political Economy* 72 (December): 537–62.

Tom, Willard K., David A. Balto, and Neil W. Averitt. 2000. "Anticompetitive Aspects of Market-Share Discounts and Other Incentives to Exclusive Dealing." *Antitrust Law Journal* 67, no. 3: 615–39.

von Weizsacker, Carl C. 1980. "A Welfare Analysis of Barriers to Entry." *Bell Journal of Economics* 11 (Spring): 399–420.

Whinston, Michael D. 1990. "Tying, Foreclosure, and Exclusion." *American Economic Review* 80, no. 4: 837–59.

DENNIS W. CARLTON
MICHAEL WALDMAN

3 | *Why Tie an Essential Good?*

Numerous important antitrust cases, such as the IBM cases of the 1970s and 1980s and the Microsoft cases of the 1990s and 2000s, alleged tying or related behavior employed for exclusionary reasons. For example, an important allegation of the *United States* v. *Microsoft* case was that Microsoft tied Internet Explorer to its Windows operating system in order to harm Netscape.[1] The standard theory of tie-ins implies that the tying or tying-like behavior took place in these cases in settings in which tying for exclusionary reasons does not result in increased profitability. This introduces the following question: Does standard theory correctly identify the circumstances in which a monopolist will tie for exclusionary reasons? In this chapter we argue that the answer is no and discuss various reasons based on our own recent research into why a monopolist in these types of settings might tie in order to exclude competitors.

Starting in the 1950s, a number of authors typically associated with the Chicago School argued that a monopolist of a primary good would never have an incentive to tie a complementary good for exclusionary reasons because all the potential monopoly profits could be captured through the

1. *United States* v. *Microsoft Corp.,* C.A. 98-1232 (2000). See Gilbert and Katz (2001) and Whinston (2001) for discussions of this case.

primary good monopoly. Michael Whinston considers this argument formally and derives a set of conditions under which the argument is valid and also conditions under which the argument breaks down.[2] In particular, he finds that the Chicago School argument is correct when the monopolist's primary good is essential, that is, it is required for all uses of the complementary good. However, if the product is not essential, then tying can be profitable because of the possibility of capturing the profits associated with the use of the complementary good for which the monopolist's primary good is not essential.

The puzzle here is that this set of results does not match well with various important cases involving tying or tying-like behavior. Think of, for example, the 1970s *United States* v. *IBM* case.[3] One of the allegations in that case was that IBM designed its mainframe computers in a manner that made it difficult for other firms' peripherals, that is, complementary products, to connect with IBM's machines.[4] This is similar to a tie-in in that if a consumer cannot use another firm's peripherals, then it is as if these consumers were contractually obligated to purchase peripherals only from IBM. The puzzle here is that, according to Whinston's argument, this will only be profitable for exclusionary reasons if the result of the behavior was that IBM increased its profits in selling its peripherals for use with rivals' mainframe computers. But for many of the peripherals, these other markets were small or nonexistent, and there was also little evidence that IBM employed this tying-like behavior to increase the profitability of its peripheral products in these other markets. Similarly, the Microsoft cases also do not easily fit Whinston's findings.[5]

The traditional literature on tying does provide a few possible answers to this puzzle based on the idea that the tying did not serve an exclusionary purpose, but we feel these traditional answers do not correspond well with the facts of the relevant cases. Specifically, Whinston's analysis assumes that the

2. Whinston (1990).

3. See *United States* v. *IBM*, C.A. 69-200 (1969), and *In re International Business Machines Corp.*, 687 F.2d 591 (2d Cir. 1982).

4. For discussions of the *United States* v. *IBM* case, see Soma (1976); McAdams (1982); Fisher, McGowan, and Greenwood (1983).

5. Other related cases include *MCI* v. *AT&T*, where the behavior concerned AT&T's refusal to allow MCI to connect its microwave system to AT&T's nationwide telephone network, and *Jefferson Parish*, where the Supreme Court ruled that a monopoly hospital could not force its surgical patients to use its own anesthesiologists. See *MCI Communications* v. *American Telephone and Telegraph Co.*, 746 F.2d 168 (2d Cir 1984), and *Jefferson Parrish Hospital District No. 2* v. *Hyde*, 466 U.S. 2 (1984).

goods are consumed in fixed proportions, that is, he assumes that the demand is for systems composed of one primary unit and one complementary unit. Therefore one possible answer to the puzzle is to assume variable proportions. Allowing variable proportions introduces two reasons why a primary-good monopolist might tie even though the primary product is essential. First, tying may be used to price discriminate, as in the standard metered-sales argument. Second, tying may be used to avoid standard inefficiencies that arise when complementary goods are sold separately and one is produced by a monopolist while the other is supplied competitively. The problem with these arguments is that many of the relevant cases fit more naturally the fixed-proportions rather than the variable-proportions assumption.

This chapter discusses two answers to this puzzle that we have formally developed in recent papers. The first focuses on the idea that the essential nature of the monopolist's primary product may not be permanent.[6] We consider two-period settings in which there is a monopolist that can produce primary and complementary goods, where the products are only consumed as a system consisting of one primary and one complementary unit. There is a potential entrant that can enter the complementary market in either period but can only enter the primary market in the second period, where the two firms have identical primary products but the entrant's complementary product is superior. Given that the two goods can only be consumed together, the monopolist's primary good is essential in the first period, but because of potential primary market entry in the second period, it is not necessarily essential in the second.

Our analysis of this setting yields that, in the presence of either entry costs or complementary good network externalities, the monopolist may tie in the first period in order to preserve its monopoly position in the second. That is, even though the monopolist's primary product in the first period is essential for all uses of the complementary good, the monopolist may increase its profits by tying. In this model the return for the alternative producer to enter the primary market in the second period is that it increases the surplus the alternative producer captures in the second period from having entered the complementary market in either the first or second periods. In the presence, for example, of entry costs, tying reduces the alternative producer's return from complementary market entry, and if the firm does not enter the com-

---

6. Carlton and Waldman (2002).

plementary market, then in this model it also does not enter the primary market.

The second answer to the puzzle is developed in a 2005 paper that focuses on the idea that a monopolist may tie when its primary product is essential in settings characterized by durable goods, upgrades, and switching costs.[7] We consider a two-period setting in which a monopolist produces both primary and complementary goods, the alternative producer can only produce the complementary good, the alternative producer's complementary good is superior, the two goods are only consumed together as a system, and upgrade prices are determined in the second period. Thus in this model the monopolist's primary good is essential in both periods. Products in this model are durable so that a good purchased in the first period can be used for consumption in the second. But there are also complementary good upgrades and switching costs. Upgrades mean that each firm can invest in research and development at the beginning of the second period and produce a higher quality complementary good in the second period. Switching costs mean that a consumer derives a higher gross benefit in the second period from consuming a complementary unit produced by the same firm that produced the complementary unit consumed by the individual in the first.[8]

Our analysis of this model indicates that tying can be optimal for the monopolist even though the monopolist's primary good is essential in both periods. Consider, for example, what happens in this model when there are upgrades but no switching costs. If firms sell, as oppose to lease, their products, then in the second period, the only sales are those of the upgraded complementary good. This means that if the monopolist is not the seller of the upgraded complementary product in the second period, then the monopolist has limited ability to capture the profits associated with the second-period upgrade value. The end result is that if the advantage of the alternative producer's complementary product is significant and the upgrade value is sufficiently large, then the monopolist ties in order to capture the profits associated with upgrading. We also show that tying is not needed when

7. Carlton and Waldman (2005c).

8. There is an extensive literature that investigates models characterized by consumer switching costs, although little of that literature focuses on the case of durable goods. Papers in this literature include Klemperer (1987, 1989) and Farrell and Shapiro (1988, 1989). See Klemperer (1995) for a survey. There is also a literature concerning the upgrade process, and much of it does focus on the case of durable goods. See, for example, Fudenberg and Tirole (1998) and related analyses in Waldman (1996) and Lee and Lee (1998).

firms can lease when there are upgrades but no switching costs; however, when there are switching costs, tying can be optimal even when leasing is possible.

One reason we think our results concerning durable goods are of interest is that many of the cases of tying in which the tying product is essential fit quite well with the features of our durable goods analysis. For example, consider Microsoft. Microsoft sells products that are durable, and the situation is also characterized by complementary product upgrades and switching costs, where the switching costs are a function of the learning-by-doing associated with many of its products. The previous literature indicates that Microsoft has no need to tie since it should be able to capture all the potential profits through its pricing of Windows. In contrast, our analysis shows that Microsoft must tie in order to capture all the profits associated with complementary goods.

Overall, although theoretical possibility is not proof that our explanations correctly describe the rationale for tying in situations like the IBM and Microsoft cases, our results refute the position that economic theory does not support tying for exclusionary reasons in these types of cases. Despite this, however, we are wary of aggressive use of antitrust to attack tie-in sales. Tying in real-world markets to promote efficiency is pervasive. Furthermore, the courts have great difficulty reliably identifying the motivations for ties. Thus we believe a policy of frequent intervention is likely to decrease rather than increase welfare because the negative effects due to reductions in efficiency-based tying are likely to outweigh any positive effects due to reductions in exclusionary tying.

Standard View of Tying and Essential Products

This section first examines the Chicago School argument concerning the return to tying. It then discusses the work of Whinston, which formally investigates the Chicago School perspective and shows that whether or not that argument applies depends on whether the monopolist's primary product is essential.[9]

9. All references to Whinston's work in this section refer to his paper published in 1990 in the *American Economic Review* (Whinston 1990).

Starting in the 1950s, a number of authors typically associated with the Chicago School argued that a monopolist of a primary good would never have an incentive to tie a complementary good to the monopolized primary good because the primary-good monopoly allows the firm to capture all the potential monopoly profits.[10] The basic idea here is that since the firm is a monopolist in the primary-good market and the goods are complements, the firm can sell the products individually and raise the price of the primary good to capture the surplus value associated with the complementary product.

To see the logic of the Chicago School argument, consider the profitability of a monopolist of shoes versus the profitability of a monopolist of right shoes when left shoes are supplied competitively. Let $P = A - bX$ be the demand for pairs of shoes, where P is the market price, X is the quantity, and A and b are positive constants. Let c be the constant marginal cost for producing a shoe and assume there are no fixed costs of production. Given this cost structure, if left shoes are supplied by a competitive industry, then the zero-profit condition associated with competition yields that the market price for a left shoe is c.

In the absence of any transactions costs or other efficiency-based reasons for tying, there is no reason for a right-shoe monopolist to tie and become a monopolist of pairs of shoes. To see this, suppose a monopolist of right shoes decided to tie and in this way become a monopolist of pairs of shoes. Setting marginal revenue equal to marginal cost yields $A - 2bX = 2c$, which, in turn, yields $X = (A - 2c)/2b$ and $P = c + (A/2)$. Profits thus equal $PX - 2cX = [(A - 2c)/2][(A - 2c)/2b] = (A - 2c)^2/4b$.

Now suppose the monopolist does not tie. Because consumers can acquire left shoes at a per unit price of c, the demand for right shoes faced by the right-shoe monopolist is given by $P' = (A - c) - bX$, where P' denotes the right-shoe price and X now denotes the number of right shoes sold. Equating marginal revenue and marginal cost now yields $(A - c) - 2bX = C$ or $X = (A - 2c)/2b$ and $P' = A/2$. In turn, profits equal $P'X - cX = [(A/2) - c][(A - 2c)/2b] = (A - 2c)^2/4b$. That is, as indicated, profits are unchanged when the right-shoe monopolist ties and becomes a monopolist of pairs of shoes. Intuitively, what happens in this example is that since moving from a monopolist of right shoes to a monopolist of pairs of shoes simply paral-

10. See, for example, Director and Levi (1956); Bowman (1957); Posner (1976); Bork (1978).

lel shifts up by the amount c demand, marginal revenue, and marginal cost, the result is no change in profits.

The Chicago School argument clearly shows that tying in order to extend a monopoly position to a tied-good market need not enhance monopoly profits. But the authors who put forth this argument never developed it in a way that demonstrates the generality of the argument. The left shoe–right shoe example discussed above captures the essence of some of the relevant real-world settings, but there are others in which it is not a good fit. So although the Chicago School argument was and is quite influential in terms of how individuals view tying behavior, the argument does not constitute a general argument that tying to extend a monopoly position given complementary products is never profitable.

With this in mind, in his seminal 1990 paper, Whinston set out to identify the generality of the Chicago School conclusion.[11] He considers a setting in which there is a monopolist of a primary good, there is a complementary good that can be produced by the monopolist and a single alternative producer, there are constant marginal costs of production, and an initial assumption that the goods are consumed only as a system consisting of one primary unit and one complementary unit. His first main result is that the Chicago School argument is fully general for such a setting. That is, the monopolist cannot increase its profits by tying its complementary good to its monopolized primary good, and, in fact, tying can actually hurt profitability.

To see the logic of Whinston's result, consider first a monopolist in this situation that chooses to sell individual products rather than tie.[12] Let π^* denote monopoly profits given tying and P^* denote the price the monopolist would charge for its bundled product if it ties. By selling individual products, if the monopolist sets the price for the monopolized primary good at P^* minus the marginal cost for the complementary good, and the price for the complementary good at its marginal cost, then the monopolist ensures itself profits at least equal to π^*. Hence the equilibrium strategy if the firm chooses to sell individual products must yield profits at least equal to π^*,

11. See also the earlier work of Ordover, Sykes, and Willig (1985).

12. As indicated, Whinston assumes constant marginal costs. Although we have not seen the result shown formally, we believe the argument that follows and thus Whinston's conclusion generalize to the cases of upward sloping and downward sloping marginal costs for the complementary good. We believe this is also the case when the monopolist does not have a constant marginal cost for the primary good, given some small changes in the setup of the model.

which means there is no return to tying. Note that, in fact, tying in this case could hurt monopoly profitability since tying means the firm captures none of the potential surplus associated with the alternative producer's complementary good, whereas selling individual products leaves open the possibility that the monopolist captures some of this surplus.

In this first analysis, the monopolist's primary good is essential, that is, it is required for all uses of the complementary good. After demonstrating the result described above, Whinston then conducts a second analysis that violates this assumption. In this second analysis, there are two uses for the complementary good. As before, the first use is as a component in systems consisting of one primary and one complementary unit. The second use is as a separate and distinct market (market B) in which consumers have a direct valuation for the complementary good and the good is not used with the primary good.

If market B is characterized by constant returns to scale and perfect competition, then there is no return to the monopolist for tying. The reason is that if the monopolist ties and induces some exit of alternative producers of the complementary good, there is no effect on the equilibrium price in the B market and thus no effect on the profits the monopolist derives in the B market. But if we move away from constant returns to scale and perfect competition, then tying to increase profitability in the B market becomes possible. For example, suppose there is a single alternative producer of B who is characterized by fixed costs of production. By tying, the monopolist stops the alternative producer from selling complementary units to be used in systems in combination with the monopolist's primary units, and this reduction in sales can cause the alternative producer to exit complementary good production because it is no longer able to cover its fixed costs. In turn, exit means increased profitability for the monopolist because it now monopolizes sales in market B.[13]

In summary, Whinston's classic analysis identifies whether the monopolist's primary product is essential as the key property that determines whether or not there can be a return for the monopolist to tie for exclusionary reasons. If the primary product is essential, that is, if the primary product is

13. Whinston also shows a second case in which a monopolist may tie a nonessential primary product in order to exclude competition. In this second analysis, there is a competitively supplied inferior substitute for the monopolist's primary product, and the monopolist ties in order to eliminate the ability of consumers to use the inferior substitute.

required for all uses of the complementary good, then there is no return to tying because as originally argued by the Chicago School authors, the monopolist can capture all potential monopoly profits through the pricing of the primary product. However, if the primary product is not essential in the sense that there is some use of the complementary good that does not require the primary good, then tying will sometimes improve profitability. The reason is that tying has the potential to increase monopoly profitability in sales of the complementary good in which the good is not used in combination with the primary good.

The puzzle associated with Whinston's result is that it does not match well with what has been observed in important real-world cases of tying for exclusionary purposes. As mentioned earlier, the most famous cases of this type are the IBM cases of the 1970s and 1980s and the recent Microsoft cases. Consider what Whinston's analysis implies. It says, for example, that in the case of IBM, for a peripheral that was only used in combination with mainframes, the firm tied or employed tying-like behavior in order to increase the profitability of selling the peripheral for use with rivals' mainframes. But this return to tying is small as long as IBM had, as was the case, a very high share of the market for mainframes. Furthermore, we know of no evidence that the profitability of IBM's peripheral sales for use with rivals' machines was substantial.

The traditional literature on tying provides two potentially related answers to this puzzle that focus on the idea that the tying did not have an exclusionary purpose, but we do not find either answer satisfactory. An important assumption in Whinston's analysis is that the primary and complementary goods are used in fixed proportions by consumers. Suppose instead that the goods were used in variable proportions, that is, suppose that consumers had a demand for a single primary unit but a variable number of complementary units. This introduces two possible reasons why a monopolist of the primary good would tie even if the primary good was essential for all uses of the complementary good.

The first is the standard argument concerning metered sales originally put forth to explain IBM's actions in an earlier case concerning the firm's tying of punch card sales to the sales of its tabulating machines.[14] In this argument

14. *IBM* v. *United States*, 298 U.S. 131 (1936). See Chen and Ross (1993) and Klein (1993) for related analyses.

consumers vary in their valuations for the monopolist's primary product, where higher valuation consumers are also more intensive users of the machine. If the monopolist cannot directly price discriminate, either because it cannot prevent resale or because it cannot identify who are the high- and who are the low-valuation consumers, then it may tie the complementary product to the sale of the primary good because this allows the firm to indirectly price discriminate. In particular, setting a high price on the complementary product and a low price on the primary product allows the firm to price discriminate, that is, the high-valuation or intensive users of the primary product pay a high overall price while the low-valuation or nonintensive users pay a low overall price.

The second argument concerning variable proportions is an efficiency-based argument.[15] Consider a setting in which the primary good is produced by a monopolist, the complementary good is competitively supplied, and there are variable proportions so that consumers choose how much of each good to consume. Because the primary good will be priced above marginal cost while competition means the complementary good will be priced at marginal cost, consumers will inefficiently consume too much of the complementary good and too little of the primary good. By tying, the monopolist can avoid this inefficiency and also potentially increase its market power. Hence tying in this case increases monopoly profits while the effect on social welfare is ambiguous.

The problem with these explanations for why a monopolist of an essential primary good might tie is that the fixed-proportions assumption seems to better describe the main relevant cases than an assumption of variable proportions. Think, for example, of the tying at the center of the recent U.S. case against Microsoft, that is, the tying of Internet Explorer with Windows. For both products consumers would typically demand either zero or one unit of the good. Thus it is hard to see how an argument based on variable proportions can explain Microsoft's actions in that case.[16]

---

15. See, for example, Malella and Nahata (1980).

16. In terms of the IBM cases, a similar argument applies concerning any specific peripheral. However, for all peripherals taken in combination, it is possible that the metered-sales argument might apply to the extent that high-valuation consumers use a larger number of different types of peripherals. Also, IBM did tie maintenance in that case, and this behavior is consistent with the efficiency-based argument just discussed.

Preserving Market Power in the Tying-Good Market

One reason a monopolist of a (currently) essential primary good might tie is to preserve its monopoly position in the future.[17] This result can be demonstrated both under the assumption of entry costs for the complementary good and under the assumption of complementary good network externalities. Because the former argument is more straightforward, that is where we begin.

We consider a two-period setting in which there is an incumbent monopolist that can produce both primary and complementary goods. There is also a single alternative producer that can enter the complementary market in either period but can only enter the primary market in the second period, where the alternative producer has a cost of entering each market. We assume that the alternative producer's complementary product is superior to the monopolist's while the two firms' primary goods are identical. Assuming that the alternative producer's complementary good is superior means that the focus is on tying used to prohibit the entry of a superior product.

Each period is characterized by a cohort of N identical consumers who place a value V on a system composed of a primary unit and a unit of the monopolist's complementary product, while a system consisting of a primary unit and the alternative producer's complementary product is valued at $V + \Delta$. We also assume that consumers have no value on either product by itself. In combination with our assumption that the alternative producer can only enter the primary market in the second period, this means that the monopolist's primary product is essential in the first period. Following Whinston, we assume that ties are irreversible, that is, a consumer that purchases a tied product consisting of the monopolist's primary and complementary goods is not able to add the alternative producer's complementary good to his system.[18] Further, the sequence of events is such that at the beginning of the first period, the monopolist decides whether to offer tied or individual products, where the tying decision is binding for both periods. The assumption that the decision is binding for both periods is consistent with the tie's being accomplished through product design rather than contracting.

17. This section is based on the study by Carlton and Waldman (2002). Related analyses appear in Choi and Stefanadis (2001) and Nalebuff (2004).

18. See Whinston (1990).

Finally, we assume that if the alternative producer has entered either market in a specific period, then prices are determined by Bertrand competition.[19] In a period in which the alternative producer has only entered the complementary market, the assumption of Bertrand competition does not result in a unique set of prices. The specific issue is how do the prices divide the surplus associated with the alternative producer's superior complementary product across the two firms? Any division that gives each firm a positive share of the surplus is consistent with equilibrium pricing. To avoid this indeterminacy, we assume that when this situation arises, the prices that emerge evenly divide across the two sellers the surplus associated with the alternative producer's superior product. Our results work as long as each firm receives a strictly positive share of the surplus.

If the alternative producer's second-period entry cost for the primary market is prohibitively high, then there is no return to tying for the monopolist. This is simply an application of Whinston's logic described in the previous section. That is, in this case the monopolist can ensure itself profits over the two periods equal to the profits from tying by selling individual products; in each period it would set the price for the complementary good at marginal cost and the price for the primary good at the optimal bundle price minus the complementary good price. In turn, since there is a strategy associated with selling individual products that yields the same profits as tying, the equilibrium outcome associated with selling individual products must be at least as high as with tying.

Next consider what happens when the alternative producer's cost of entering the primary market is small but positive. Here we show that if the alternative producer's cost of entering the complementary market falls in an intermediate range, then the monopolist ties and deters the alternative producer from ever entering either market. Note that if this entry cost is below this intermediate range, then tying does not stop second-period entry, so there is no reason for the monopolist to tie. On the other hand, if this entry cost is above this intermediate range, then the alternative producer never enters either market, even if the monopolist sells individual products, so again there is no return to tying. But if the entry cost falls in the intermedi-

---

19. Bertrand competition means that each firm takes the other firms' price or prices as given in choosing its own prices. In the case of single-product firms and identical products, this assumption leads to marginal cost pricing.

ate range, then the alternative producer does not enter either market if the monopolist ties and enters both markets, if the monopolist sells individual products. Given that in our model the primary market monopoly is very valuable for the monopolist, the result in this case is that the monopolist ties to preserve its primary market monopoly in the second period.

The logic for why tying deters entry into both markets when the alternative producer's complementary-market entry cost falls in the intermediate range is as follows. In our model, if the alternative producer does not enter the complementary market in either period, then it does not enter the primary market in the second period since Bertrand competition and identical products mean that primary-market entry by itself necessarily yields negative profits for the firm. But if the alternative producer enters the complementary market in either the first or second periods, then it enters the primary market in the second. In this case the return to primary-market entry is that in the second period, the alternative producer captures all—rather than half—of the surplus associated with its superior complementary product.

Suppose the monopolist ties. This stops the alternative producer from selling complementary units in the first period since there is no primary product available to be used in combination with the alternative producer's complementary product. This lowers the return to the alternative producer of complementary-market entry. Furthermore, when the alternative producer's entry cost falls in the intermediate range, this reduction moves the alternative producer from a situation in which it enters the complementary market in the first period—when the monopolist sells individual products— to one in which it does not enter the complementary market in either period when the monopolist ties. In turn, as stated, if the alternative producer does not enter the complementary market, then it also does not enter the primary market, and so the monopolist preserves its monopoly position in the primary market in the second period.

To make our argument more concrete from a real-world standpoint, suppose counterfactually that in the 1970s IBM had a monopoly on computer mainframes while Memorex, the alternative producer, had a monopoly on disk drives used in combination with mainframes. Since a mainframe was essential for using a disk drive, most models of pricing would suggest that some of the value that consumers placed on the Memorex disk drives would be captured by IBM in the pricing of its mainframes. This means that Memorex would have had a high incentive to enter the mainframe market because, in addition to any profits it might capture in the mainframe market, entry into that market would allow it to capture more of the surplus associated with its own disk drives. Hence, if IBM were interested in preserving its mainframe monopoly, which it surely was, then it would have had an incentive to not have a peripheral market, such as the one for disk drives, dominated by a potential rival in the mainframe market. One way it could have avoided this outcome would have been by tying its own peripherals to its mainframes.[20]

The above discussion describes our analysis given entry costs for the complementary good. We also show similar results when there are no entry costs for the complementary good but rather complementary-good network externalities, that is, consumer i's gross benefit is higher when more individuals consume the same complementary product as consumer i. The logic here is that by tying, the monopolist again stops the alternative producer from selling any complementary units in the first period. In turn, because of network externalities, the reduction in first-period sales makes the alternative producer's complementary product less attractive in the second period. The end result is that tying can stop the alternative producer from selling complementary units in both periods, and similar to the entry-cost analysis, the monopolist does not enter the primary market in the second period if it sells no complementary units.

One interesting difference between the two analyses concerns real ties versus virtual ties achieved through pricing. In the latter situation, the monopolist prices the complementary good low enough that it is as if the two goods were tied together. In our first or entry-cost analysis, real ties were required to deter entry. The reason is that there is a time-inconsistency problem concerning virtual ties. That is, because pricing is determined after the alternative producer's entry decision, the strategy for the monopolist of setting a low postentry price on the complementary good, in order to deter alternative-producer entry, is not credible. In the network-externalities case, however, the key for the monopolist is not to stop entry but rather to stop the alternative producer from selling complementary units in the first period.

20. Frequently IBM did not literally tie its peripherals to its mainframes. But it was alleged that it acted in a manner that disadvantaged rivals' peripheral products, such as frequent mainframe design changes that necessitated design changes in the peripheral for it to work effectively with the mainframe. Our argument explains this behavior.

Therefore, low pricing by the monopolist for the complementary product is a credible and feasible strategy.

One aspect of our second model is that a variant can be used to capture the U.S. Justice Department's argument in the Microsoft case concerning the "applications barrier to entry."[21] There were three steps to their argument. First, firms could not enter the operating-systems market because of the lack of applications programs written for rival systems. Second, if a rival browser were sufficiently popular, programmers would have an incentive to write applications that would run on the rival browser. This, in turn, means that a successful rival browser had the potential to evolve into a substitute for Windows and thus threaten the Windows monopoly. Third, Microsoft had an incentive to stop this from occurring, and so it tied Windows to Internet Explorer in order to reduce Netscape Navigator's market share and in this way protect its operating-systems monopoly.

A slight variant of our network-externalities model captures this argument. The main differences are that here we assume the alternative producer can enter the primary market in period two only if it sold complementary units in period one, and we further assume that consumers can undo ties or, equivalently, ties are reversible. The most interesting result here is that for every parameterization in which tying is optimal, a virtual tie achieved through pricing is just as effective as a real tie achieved through contracting or product design. (In our main network-externalities analysis, this was the case for only some of the relevant parameterizations.)

This finding matches well with what actually happened. In the actual case, Microsoft tied Windows and Internet Explorer and forbade computer manufacturers to remove the browser from computers. In 1998, however, during the Justice Department's contempt proceedings concerning this behavior, Microsoft eliminated the tie and reduced the price of Explorer to zero. Consistent with our analysis that in such situations virtual ties achieved through pricing should be as effective as real ties, the change in Microsoft's behavior did not seem to have any negative effect on the rate at which Microsoft increased its market share in the browser market.

21. *United States* v. *Microsoft Corp.*, C.A. 98-1232, Complaint (1998).

Capturing Surplus in the Tied-Good
Market When Products Are Durable

In this section we show that one reason a monopolist of an essential primary good may tie is that tying may allow the firm to capture additional profits in the tied-good market when goods are durable and upgrade prices are determined after the initial period.[22] In particular, it is the presence of product upgrades and consumer switching costs, which are standard in durable goods markets, that makes tying in such markets a valuable tool. Our analysis considers both what happens when there are product upgrades and no switching costs and what happens given upgrades and switching costs.

Again we consider a two-period setting in which there is an incumbent monopolist that can produce both primary and complementary goods, where now both products are durable. That is, a product produced in the first period can be used for consumption in both periods. We also assume a single alternative producer that can produce the complementary good but not the primary good, and as before, the alternative producer's complementary good is superior to the monopolist's complementary good. Given the additional assumption that goods are only consumed in systems consisting of one primary unit and one complementary unit, in this model the monopolist's primary good is essential for all uses of the complementary product in both periods.

As is the case for numerous durable goods markets, we assume that the complementary-good market is characterized by upgrades. That is, at the beginning of the second period, each firm has the option of investing in research and development and thus providing itself with the ability to produce a higher quality complementary product in the second period. In part of our analysis, we also assume that the complementary good is characterized by consumer switching costs. That is, in the second period, a consumer derives a higher benefit by consuming a system that contains a complementary unit produced by the same firm that produced the complementary unit consumed by this individual in the previous period. Note that one reason there can be consumer switching costs is that the complementary good entails learning-by-doing.

---

22. See Carlton and Waldman (2005c).

We assume there is a single cohort of N identical consumers who live for two periods.[23] In period one each consumer derives a gross benefit of V_M from a system in which both components are produced by the monopolist, while the individual receives V_A, where $V_A > V_M$, if he consumes a system in which the complementary good is produced by the alternative producer. In the second period, the only changes are that gross benefit goes up by λ if the complementary good consumed is an upgraded unit, and when there are switching costs, gross benefit goes up by Δ if the complementary good consumed is produced by the same firm that produced the complementary unit the individual consumed in the previous period.

As in the previous model, at the beginning of the first period, the monopolist chooses whether to offer tied or individual products, and this choice is binding for both periods. If the monopolist chooses to tie, then consumers are not able to add to their systems a complementary unit produced by the alternative producer, that is, ties are irreversible. Note, however, if a consumer purchases a tied product from the monopolist in the first period, the consumer in the second period is able to add an upgraded complementary unit produced by the monopolist. This last assumption matches well with how tying worked in both the IBM and Microsoft cases.

First consider what happens when there are complementary-good upgrades but no switching costs. Our analysis shows that if firms sell rather than lease their products, then the monopolist will tie given that the alternative producer's complementary product is sufficiently superior and the value consumers place on the upgrade is sufficiently high. The logic for why a high-upgrade value is important is that the monopolist cannot capture the value of the upgrade through the first-period price for the primary product. As a result, if the monopolist sells individual products, then in the second period, the alternative producer sells upgraded complementary units and captures profits due to the upgrade value. Hence, if this upgrade value is sufficiently high, then the monopolist increases its profits by tying since tying means that the alternative producer cannot sell complementary units, and so the monopolist captures the profits due to the upgrade value.[24]

23. The time-inconsistency problem concerning durable goods monopolists, first identified in the work of Coase (1972) and Bulow (1982), is not a factor in our analysis because of our assumption that consumers are identical. This means that the monopolist does not face a downward sloping demand curve for its products, so downward sloping demand does not give the firm a reason to lower its price or prices in the second period.

24. The requirement that the alternative producer's complementary product is sufficiently superior

Now consider what happens in the case of upgrades only when firms can either sell or lease their products. Here we show that there is no longer a return to tying, where the basic logic of the result is an extension to a two-period setting of Whinston's original argument for why tying is not needed when the monopolist's primary good is essential. That is, by leasing individual products, upgrading in the second period, and optimally choosing prices for the leased goods in each period, the monopolist can ensure itself profits at least as high as when it ties. In fact, we show that in some equilibria in this case, the monopolist does better by leasing individual products than by tying. The reason is that in these equilibria leasing individual products allows the monopolist to capture some of the surplus associated with the alternative producer's superior complementary product, whereas tying means the monopolist does not capture any of this surplus.

Our second main analysis considers what happens when there are both upgrades and consumer switching costs. Here we show that there can be a return to tying when firms can both sell and lease their products. The key point here is that if the monopolist leases individual products, upgrades, and prices optimally, it cannot ensure itself profits at least as high as those associated with tying. In other words, Whinston's logic concerning essential goods does not apply in this case even when the firm leases. The reason is that if the alternative producer leases complementary units in the first period, then because of the switching costs, the monopolist's complementary product is a less attractive alternative in the second period. The result is that leasing individual products does not ensure that the monopolist captures profits due to the switching costs, so tying can be preferred to leasing individual products if the switching-cost profits are high.[25]

We also consider a number of extensions including the role of the reversibility of ties.[26] Following Whinston, in our main analyses we assume tying is irreversible, that is, a consumer purchasing a tied product from the monopolist cannot add the alternative producer's complementary product

---

eliminates a multiple equilibrium problem concerning who invests in the second period.

25. A key part of the argument here is that prices are assumed to be nonnegative. If we allowed strictly negative prices, then competition in terms of the first-period complementary-good price would enable the monopolist to capture second-period switching-cost profits by leasing individual products and charging a sufficiently high first-period price for the primary good.

26. The other two extensions we consider are what happens when we relax our assumption that prices must be nonnegative (see footnote 25 for a related discussion), and what happens when primary-good upgrades are incorporated into the analysis.

to his system.[27] But this assumption does not exactly match tying in the relevant real-world situations such as the Microsoft and IBM cases. In each of those cases, consumers could sometimes add an alternative producer's complementary product to their systems even when the original purchase was a tied product produced by the monopolist. So the obvious question is, how do our analyses change when we relax this assumption?

The answer is in two parts. First, if tying is completely reversible, then tying never improves monopoly profitability. The reason is that when tying is completely reversible, a tie is essentially no different than having the monopolist market its products individually and set the price of the complementary good at zero. Hence, whenever tying is useful for monopolizing the complementary-good market, the monopolist could instead accomplish its goal by marketing individual products and setting a low price on the complementary good. This result suggests that in real-world durable goods markets, we should observe a low frequency of tying to monopolize complementary-good markets when tying is completely or almost completely reversible.[28]

Second, suppose the tie is partially reversible, that is, tying either increases the cost of a consumer's adding the alternative producer's complementary good to his system or reduces the functionality of the alternative producer's product. Then tying will sometimes increase monopoly profitability.[29] The logic here is that when ties are partially reversible in the sense just described, tying is like setting a negative price on the complementary good equal to the added cost tying creates for adding the alternative producer's product to a system. Given this, consider a setting in which the primary-good monopolist would like to monopolize the complementary-good market, but a zero price for the complementary good will not achieve the goal. Then tying will enhance monopoly profits if this added cost associated with tying is sufficiently high that the firm monopolizes the complementary-good market. This result suggests that relative to the completely reversible case, in real-world durable goods markets, tying should be more common when ties are only partially reversible.

27. See Whinston (1990).
28. In the terminology used in the previous section, this is equivalent to saying that when tying is reversible, virtual ties are as effective as real ties. See Carlton and Waldman (2002).
29. The argument here is an example of the idea that firms sometimes have an incentive to behave in ways that raise rivals' costs. See Salop and Scheffman (1983, 1987) for early analyses of this idea.

What is interesting about our results concerning the reversibility of ties is that it matches quite well with what we know about the relevant cases. For example, consider Microsoft's tying. It is not simply that Microsoft ties its products. In many of the relevant examples, in addition to tying, Microsoft behaves in a manner that raises the cost of consumers' adding alternative producers' products to their systems. Specifically, Microsoft frequently integrates the code for the application directly into Windows programming code rather than have the application connect to Windows through an interface. This can raise an alternative producer's cost because it is difficult or impossible for the alternative producer to reverse engineer Microsoft's products and have the alternative producer's product interface with Windows in the same manner that Microsoft's application program does. Additionally, in other cases Microsoft keeps interfaces secret, which again has the effect of increasing alternative producers' costs or impairing the functionality of alternative producers' products. Our theoretical analysis explains why Microsoft's tying is frequently associated with these types of behavior.

There is also a close match with behavior in the IBM cases. As discussed earlier, an important allegation in the *United States* v. *IBM* case was that IBM introduced frequent design changes into its mainframe computers, which meant that alternative producers of peripherals had to make costly design changes in their products in order for them to work effectively with IBM's computers. According to Whinston's argument, to the extent that IBM had a monopoly on mainframes, this behavior would not be optimal since superior complementary products produced by rival firms can only help an essential-good monopolist. But our analysis shows this behavior can be profit maximizing. If tying was reversible when the mainframe was new, which was typically the case with IBM, then introducing these design changes could have raised rivals' costs, which our analysis indicates can be profitable because it better allows the monopolist to capture profits associated with complementary-good upgrade profits and switching-cost profits.[30]

---

30. In some instances IBM tied the complementary good when the mainframe was new and the design change served to raise rivals' costs for selling replacement parts. In other instances IBM did not tie the complementary good initially, so these design changes would have raised rivals' costs for the sale of "new" units and replacement units. Although we have not formally considered an analysis along this line, our preliminary analysis of this case suggests that results similar to the ones reported in the text apply.

Antitrust Implications

Our analyses show that tying can be used for exclusionary purposes in a wider variety of circumstances than is suggested by earlier literature on the subject. One might be tempted to conclude from this that an interventionist government policy concerning tying arrangements is justified. But we feel that such a conclusion is not, in fact, justified. Even given our results concerning exclusionary tying of essential products, we believe that the correct government stance is to require a very high hurdle for intervention.[31]

There are two main reasons why we believe that a high hurdle should be required for government intervention in tie-in cases. The first and most important reason is the prevalence of efficiency-based tying.[32] Ties driven by efficiency are pervasive. In fact, one can think of almost any product as being a bundle of individual components where most of the bundling is driven by efficiency. Examples include the packaging of left and right shoes into pairs, the fact that most cars are sold with a radio as well as tires included, and the fact that most hotels do not charge separately for rooms and maid service. With so much tying driven by efficiency, an interventionist policy is likely to do more harm than good. The basic problem is that it is difficult for the courts to reliably identify the true motivation for a tie. So a policy of intervention based on speculation concerning motivation will likely lower expected welfare, both because intervention will sometimes occur in cases where the tie was actually driven by efficiency and because firms will likely forgo instances of efficient tying for fear of prosecution. So, given the prevalence of efficiency-based tying in real-world markets, we believe intervention should be confined to cases where the evidence points unambiguously to an exclusionary rationale.

The second reason we believe in a high hurdle for government intervention in tie-in cases is that even some of the exclusionary arguments discussed in the two preceding sections have ambiguous social-welfare implications. For example, suppose the courts concluded—based on strong evidence such as internal memos and e-mails—that the motivation for a tie

---

31. See Carlton and Waldman (2005a, 2005b) for detailed discussions of our views for optimal antitrust policy concerning tie-in sales.

32. See Carlton and Perloff (2005) and Evans and Salinger (2005) for discussions of efficiency-based reasons for tying.

was the tie-in theory concerning durable goods, upgrades, and switching costs described above. Our analysis indicates that the social-welfare effects of tying in that case are ambiguous.[33] Tying can cause social welfare to fall because consumers do not have access to the alternative producer's superior complementary product, but it can also rise because when the monopolist ties, only one firm rather than two upgrades its products, resulting in a saving in research and development expenditures. Determining which impact on welfare is more significant depends on details of the setting, such as the size of research and development expenditures needed for upgrading. And because the courts cannot reliably identify the magnitudes of these types of effects, a policy of aggressive intervention by the government is problematic.

Aside from a general prescription for a high hurdle for intervention, one would also want to take into account the nature of the tie. In particular, we believe the hurdle should be higher regarding product design ties relative to ties that are accomplished through contract. The former would require intervening in the internal workings of the firm, a complicated undertaking because of effects on internal relationships and transactions that are hard to predict. On the other hand, contractual ties are determined by the market mechanism where the effects of intervention are likely to be more clear cut. Note that our suggestion here is consistent with current treatment of exclusive dealing, where courts are much more likely to intervene when the exclusivity is accomplished by contract rather than by vertical integration into retailing.

One additional issue of relevance is the effect that tying for exclusionary reasons can have on technological progress in an industry. The analyses described in the preceding sections mostly take the rate of technological progress as given. But if tying increases market power, as those analyses indicate it sometimes will, it is possible that the increased profits associated with that increased market power will raise the rate of return to innovation in the industry and in this way raise both product qualities and social welfare. This is especially relevant since various empirical studies show that in general the social rate of return to innovation exceeds the private return.[34] Despite the clear logic here, however, we have never seen this type of argument considered by courts in an antitrust case as a valid reason for allowing monopolization.

33. See also Carlton and Waldman (2005c).
34. See, for example, Mansfield and others (1977); Bernstein and Nadiri (1988); Mansfield (1991).

In summary, we believe that because of the pervasiveness of efficiency-based tying, in general there should be a very high hurdle required for government intervention in tying cases. Optimally there should be clear and convincing evidence that the tie serves an exclusionary rationale with an anticompetitive effect, plus there should be no plausible alternative efficiency rationale for the behavior. Within this basic policy, some distinction should be made between whether the tie is achieved through product design or contracting. In the product design case, the hurdle should be especially high because of the difficulties associated with intervention that directly affects the internal workings of the firm, whereas for contractual ties, policy can be closer to that employed in exclusive-dealing cases, where the typical approach is a balancing of the likely costs and benefits of intervention.

Conclusion

In his seminal analysis of 1990, Whinston showed in a one-period setting that a monopolist of a primary good would never have an incentive to tie a complementary good for exclusionary purposes if the monopolist's primary good is essential, that is, if the monopolist's primary good is required for all uses of the complementary good. Because both in the recent Microsoft cases and the famous IBM cases of the 1970s and 1980s the firm's primary product was essential or near essential for the relevant complementary goods, one might be tempted to conclude that these firms did not tie for exclusionary reasons. But based on our analyses as discussed here, we believe this conclusion is incorrect. Whinston considers one-period settings in his analysis, but our analyses have shown that his conclusion does not generalize to multiple-period settings. In particular, either because of a desire to protect the primary-good monopoly or a desire in durable goods markets to capture profits associated with complementary-good upgrades and switching costs (where the upgrade price is determined in a later period), even when the monopolist's primary good is essential for all uses of the complementary good, there can be a return for a primary-good monopolist to tie.

Despite our demonstration that tying for exclusionary reasons is more common than the previous literature suggests, we believe one needs to be cautious in terms of using our findings to justify aggressive governmental intervention in tying behavior. First, tying for efficiency reasons is commonplace, and it is difficult for the courts to identify whether any specific instance of tying is driven by an efficiency or an exclusionary motive. Thus, in the absence of clear-cut evidence supporting exclusionary reasons for tying, government intervention is likely to reduce expected welfare, both by intervening when the tie is efficient and making firms with efficiency-based motives for tying less likely to engage in the behavior. Second, even when the behavior clearly has an exclusionary motive, the relevant theoretical analyses indicate that the social-welfare effects are frequently ambiguous and depend on details of the situation that the courts are unlikely to be able to identify in a reliable manner.

We believe our analyses provide the most plausible explanations for Microsoft's behavior and the behavior of IBM in an earlier era. In both cases one of the main concerns was how the behavior of the firm affected the rate of innovation and technological progress in the industry. Our analyses either take the rate of technological progress as given or endogenize it in a very limited manner. We believe, therefore, that the most interesting way to extend our analyses is to incorporate endogenous quality and innovation choices into the models.[35] Doing so has the potential to improve in a significant way our understanding of the social welfare implications of tying for exclusionary reasons that takes place in real-world settings.

---

35. See Choi (1996, 2004) for earlier analyses of tying where technological progress is determined endogenously.

References

Bernstein, Jeffrey I., and M. Ishaq Nadiri. 1988. "Interindustry R&D Spillovers, Rates of Return, and Production in High-Tech Industries." *American Economic Review* 78, no. 2: 429–34.

Bork, Robert H. 1978. *The Antitrust Paradox: A Policy at War with Itself.* New York: Basic Books.

Bowman, William S. 1957. "Tying Arrangements and the Leverage Problem." *Yale Law Review* 67, no. 1: 19–36.

Bulow, Jeremy. 1982. "Durable Goods Monopolists." *Journal of Political Economy* 90, no. 2: 314–32.

Carlton, Dennis W., and Jeffrey M. Perloff. 2005. *Modern Industrial Organization.* 4th ed. New York: Addison Wesley.

Carlton, Dennis W., and Michael Waldman. 2002. "The Strategic Use of Tying to Preserve and Create Market Power in Evolving Industries." *RAND Journal of Economics* 33, no. 2: 194–220.

———. 2005a. "How Economics Can Improve Antitrust Doctrine towards Tie-In Sales." *Competition Policy International* 1, no. 1: 27–40.

———. 2005b. "Theories of Tying and Implications for Antitrust." Mimeo. Cornell University.

———. 2005c. "Tying, Upgrades, and Switching Costs in Durable Goods Markets." Working Paper 11407. Cambridge, Mass.: National Bureau of Economic Research.

Chen, Zhigi, and Thomas Ross.1993. "Refusals to Deal, Price Discrimination, and Independent Service Organizations." *Journal of Economics and Management Strategy* 2, no. 4: 593–614.

Choi, Jay P. 1996. "Preemptive R&D, Rent Dissipation, and the 'Leverage Theory.'" *Quarterly Journal of Economics* 111, no. 4: 1153–81.

———. 2004. "Tying and Innovation: A Dynamic Analysis of Tying Arrangements." *Economic Journal* 114, no. 492: 83–101.

Choi, Jay P., and Christodoulos Stefanadis. 2001. "Tying, Investment, and the Dynamic Leverage Theory." *RAND Journal of Economics* 32, no. 1: 52–71.

Coase, Ronald H. 1972. "Durability and Monopoly." *Journal of Law and Economics* 15, no. 1: 143–49.

Director, Aaron, and Edward Levi. 1956. "Law and the Future: Trade Regulation." *Northwestern University Law Review* 51, no. 2: 281–96.

Evans, David S., and Michael A. Salinger. 2005. "Why Do Firms Bundle and Tie? Evidence from Competitive Markets and Implications for Tying Law." *Yale Journal on Regulation* 22, no. 1: 38–89.

Farrell, Joseph, and Carl Shapiro. 1988. "Dynamic Competition with Switching Costs." *RAND Journal of Economics* 19, no. 1: 123–37.

———. 1989. "Optimal Contracts with Lock-In." *American Economic Review* 79, no. 1: 51–68.

Fisher, Franklin M., John T. McGowan, and Joen E. Greenwood. 1983. *Folded, Spindled, and Mutilated: Economic Analysis and U.S. v. IBM.* MIT Press.

Fudenberg, Drew, and Jean Tirole. 1998. "Upgrades, Tradeins, and Buybacks." *RAND Journal of Economics* 29, no. 2: 235–58.

Gilbert, Richard J., and Michael L. Katz. 2001. "An Economist's Guide to *U.S. v. Microsoft.*" *Journal of Economic Perspectives* 15, no. 2: 25–44.

Klein, Benjamin. 1993. "Market Power in Antitrust: Economic Analysis after *Kodak.*" *Supreme Court Economic Review* 3: 43–92.

Klemperer, Paul. 1987. "Markets with Consumer Switching Costs." *Quarterly Journal of Economics* 102, no. 2: 375–94.

———. 1989. "Price Wars Caused by Switching Costs." *Review of Economic Studies* 56, no. 3: 405–20.

———. 1995. "Competition When Consumers Have Switching Costs: An Overview with Applications to Industrial Organization, Macroeconomics, and International Trade." *Review of Economic Studies,* 62, no. 4: 515–39.

Lee, In Ho, and Jonghwa Lee. 1998. "A Theory of Economic Obsolescence." *Journal of Industrial Economics* 46, no. 3: 383–401.

Malella, Parthasaradhi, and Babu Nahata. 1980. "Theory of Vertical Control with Variable Proportions." *Journal of Political Economy* 88, no. 5: 1009–25.

Mansfield, Edwin. 1991. "Social Returns from R&D: Findings, Methods and Limitations." *Research Technology Management* 34, no. 6: 24–27.

Mansfield, Edwin, and others. 1977. "Social and Private Rates of Return from Industrial Innovations." *Quarterly Journal of Economics* 92, no. 2: 223–40.

McAdams, Alan K. 1982. "The Computer Industry." In *The Structure of American Industry,* 6th ed., edited by Walter Adams, pp. 249–97. New York: Macmillan.

Nalebuff, Barry. 2004. "Bundling as an Entry Barrier." *Quarterly Journal of Economics* 119, no. 1: 159–87.

Ordover, Janusz A., Alan O. Sykes, and Robert D. Willig. 1985. "Nonprice Anticompetitive Behavior by Dominant Firms towards the Producers of Complementary Products." In *Antitrust and Regulation: Essays in Memory of John J. McGowan,* edited by Franklin M. Fisher, pp. 315–30. MIT Press.

Posner, Richard A. 1976. *Antitrust Law, An Economic Perspective.* University of Chicago Press.

Salop, Steven C., and David Scheffman. 1983. "Raising Rivals' Costs." *American Economic Review* 73, no. 2: 267–71.

———. 1987. "Cost-Raising Strategies." *Journal of Industrial Economics* 36, no. 1: 19–34.

Soma, John T. 1976. *The Computer Industry.* Lexington, Mass.: Lexington Books.

Waldman, Michael. 1996. "Planned Obsolescence and the R&D Decision." *RAND Journal of Economics* 27, no. 3: 583–95.

Whinston, Michael D. 1990. "Tying, Foreclosure, and Exclusion." *American Economic Review* 80, no. 4: 837–59.

———. 2001. "Exclusivity and Tying in *U.S.* v. *Microsoft*: What We Know, and Don't Know." *Journal of Economic Perspectives* 15, no. 2: 63–80.

DAVID S. EVANS

4 | Tying: The Poster Child for Antitrust Modernization

Tying is an area of antitrust in desperate need of modernization. First, tying is an utterly common business practice in competitive markets. That distinguishes this practice from all other practices subject to per se prohibitions and from many other practices, such as pricing below cost, that are considered suspect under a rule of reason analysis.[1] The Supreme Court recently recognized this point in its unanimous decision in *Illinois Tool Works:* "Many tying arrangements, even those involving patents and requirements ties, are fully consistent with a free, competitive market."[2]

Second, there is no support in modern economics for either a general per se prohibition against tying or the particular test adopted by the Supreme Court in 1984 in *Jefferson Parish Hospital District No. 2* v. *Hyde.*[3] Economists recognize that tying results in efficiencies that benefit consumers although tying could be used, in particular situations, for anticompetitive purposes.

This article builds on research the author has done with Christian Ahlborn, Jorge Padilla, and Michael Salinger. He appreciates comments and suggestions from Christian Ahlborn, Howard Chang, Robert Hahn, and Anne Layne-Farrar and excellent research support from Nadia Hussaini, and Sannu Shrestha.

1. There is not much empirical evidence about whether minimum resale price maintenance would be common in competitive markets, as it is subject to per se condemnation.
2. *Illinois Tool Works* v. *Independent Ink, Inc.,* 547 U.S. ____ (2006).
3. *Jefferson Parish,* 466 U.S. 2 (1984).

There is no basis for singling tying out for per se condemnation from among the range of possible unilateral practices.

Third, only deference to precedence stopped the Supreme Court from subjecting tying to a rule of reason inquiry in *Jefferson Parish*. Four judges wanted to go to with the rule of reason. The five-judge majority recognized that tying was often procompetitive, but they could not bring themselves to break with many decades of hostility toward tying.

Fourth, it is the only unilateral practice by businesses, other than minimum resale price maintenance, that is the subject of a per se prohibition under the Sherman Act.[4] In the last quarter century, the courts have gradually subjected all other unilateral practices to a rule of reason inquiry that considers, among other matters, whether the practice harms consumers on the one hand and whether it generates efficiencies on the other hand. The archaic per se rule against tying is a remnant of a now-distant past in which economic analysis had little role in antitrust laws.

This chapter establishes the four points above. The first section documents the pervasiveness of tying in competitive markets. The second section examines the modern economic understanding of the procompetitive and possibly anticompetitive explanations for tying. This is followed by a review of the *Jefferson Parish* decision and some of the prior and subsequent case law. The final section compares the evolution of tying doctrine to that of other unilateral practices, arguing that the courts should abandon *Jefferson Parish* in favor of the rule of reason or that Congress should mandate this result as part of its ongoing consideration of modernizing the antitrust laws.

Tying Is a Common Business Practice

Most products are bundles of features that could be and sometimes are provided separately.[5] Consider a morning in the life of a typical consumer. Her alarm clock goes off—this might be a radio alarm clock or the one on her mobile phone. From her doorstep she gets the *Washington Post*, which

4. I use "unilateral" to refer to single-firm practices such as tying, predation, and vertical restraints, whose potential for anticompetitive effects comes from eliminating competition from other firms. In contrast, the potential anticompetitive effects from collusive practices such as price fixing come from lessening the vitality of competition from the firm's party to the agreement. I do not mean unilateral in the sense of an absence of an agreement that is subject to section 1 of the Sherman Antitrust Act of 1890.

5. Seabright (2002); Salinger (2005); Adams and Yellen (1976); Bakos and Brynjolfsson (1999).

includes national and international news, sports, perhaps local Virginia news, and arts. For breakfast she has a bowl of Apple Cinnamon Cheerios, though she has to add the milk herself. She turns her television on to watch CNN; she skips past House and Garden TV, which she must take as part of her cable package but never watches. Then she steps into her SUV and turns on the radio, which came with the car, and if she does not know where she is going, perhaps even uses the built-in GPS navigation system. Bundling does not cease when she gets to her office. The building probably includes security services, cleaning, and other amenities. She boots up her computer, which is a bundle of an operating system, applications software, a computer chip, and perhaps a DVD player. When our subject, who is a surgeon, schedules her patients for surgery, they receive a bundle of services from the hospital, including nursing, anesthesiologists, and meals.

In all these cases, firms are making two related decisions. The first concerns how they design their products. What should be included and how should the parts interrelate? The second concerns which products to offer. Should the firm offer only one product or should it offer several with different combinations of features? The answers to these questions depend on the demand for different product configurations and the cost of providing these to consumers.

Product Design and Offers

To illustrate the decisions that firms make about how to design their products and what products to offer to consumers, consider a simple case in which there are two components *A* and *B*. Each is valuable to consumers in its own right.[6] The possible products are listed in table 4-1. Three cases are particularly important:

—*Components selling* occurs when the firm offers *A* and *B* separately (cars and bicycle racks).

—*Pure bundling* is when the firm only offers *A* and *B* together as the bundled product *AB* (men's laced shoes).

---

6. For more detail on this model, see Evans and Salinger (2005).

Table 4-1. *Products That Can Be Sold Based on Two Components*

Possible product combinations[a]	A	B	AB
1. Components selling	X	X	
2. Components selling	X		
3. Components selling		X	
4. Pure bundling-tie			X
5. Tied mixed bundling	X		X
6. Tied mixed bundling		X	X
7. Full mixed bundling	X	X	X

Source: Based on the model of Evans and Salinger (2005).
a. See text for explanation of terms.

—*Mixed bundling* refers to when the firm offers the bundle *AB* and either or both of its components *A* and *B* (the Sunday *New York Times* and the *New York Times Book Review*).

With two components, there are three possible "products" and seven possible product configurations, as shown in table 4-1. The number of products and configurations increases exponentially with the number of components. Thus with three components there are seven possible products and 127 possible product configurations.

It is useful to introduce a legal concept of bundling called a *tie* at this point (I will return to this when discussing the possible anticompetitive uses of bundling). A product configuration is said to involve a tie when it is possible to get one component only as part of a bundle. That is the case with product configurations 4 through 6 in table 4-1. Pure bundling necessarily involves a tie. Mixed bundling involves a tie when it is not possible to get one of the components. Generally, antitrust policy concerns itself only in those situations when buyers can get a tied component only by taking another component for which the firm has market power.

Firms make different decisions on product designs and offers within the same industries. Some may offer only components while others may offer only bundles and still others may engage in mixed bundling. Consider the most popular midsized automobiles sold in the United States: Ford Taurus, Honda Accord, and Toyota Camry. The Accord comes in six models that have between none and two options. The Camry has three models with between nine and twelve options. And the Taurus has four models with between three and thirteen options. Across different types of cars, there is even greater variation. Porsche is famous for having an enormous number of options that allow purchasers to customize their cars. All of these automobile makers, however, include tires on their cars. They purchase these from tire manufacturers, and none sells tires separately.[7]

The framework above can also be used to think about another form of bundling: selling multiple units of a product or other volume-based arrangements. The components are the individual units of the product. A pure bundle would be a fixed number of units—say, a package containing 100 units—and mixed bundling would entail different package sizes—for example, 25, 100, and 500 units.

Reducing Producer and Consumer Costs

Bundling decisions affect costs for both producers and consumers.[8] In both cases it is useful to divide these into costs that vary with each unit—*marginal costs*—and costs that are lumpy over a range of units—*fixed costs*.

PRODUCERS. For producers multiple offerings can raise the fixed costs of production and sales in several ways. There may be diseconomies of scope from producing multiple separate products. For example, studies of automobile manufacturing have found that making many options available increases what are called *complexity costs*. Maintaining and managing different SKUs (stock keeping units) also costs money. Separate products require separate packaging and shelf space, each of which raises costs.[9] Marginal costs also vary for some products. It is cheaper to produce one pill that contains both headache and pain reliever medicine than to produce two different pills.

It is also possible that there are diseconomies in both fixed and marginal costs of offering components together. Combining features may increase costs directly by making these products more complex and much harder to make. And complexity may have indirect effects as well, such as raising the likelihood of products breaking down, raising support costs for customers, and increasing the costs of repair. The marriage of computers and automo-

7. Evans and Salinger (2005, p. 79, note 6).
8. Rey, Seabright, and Tirole (2001[revised 2002]). See also Evans and Salinger (2004).
9. Evans and Salinger (2004).

biles is an example. Owners of Dodge 2001 minivans have, according to the *New York Times*, "posted anguished cries . . . about electronic gremlins that stop windows from rolling all the way up, that unexpectedly dim the interior lights, that drain batteries or that make engines sputter."[10]

CONSUMERS. Consumers may realize savings when getting products together, assuming they value them at all. If you like to read about sports and arts every day, it is cheaper to get a newspaper with both. And if you have a cold and a headache, it is more convenient to get a single package of pills. Letting the producer make choices for you saves you time as well. When we go to the hospital for surgery, most of us would prefer to leave most of the choices of the components to the experts rather than do it ourselves. Downloadable music lets consumers pick individual songs for their collections, but many might prefer the bundles the artists and publishers put together themselves. Choice is costly because it takes time and effort to make informed decisions, ones that others may be able to do more efficiently. More generally, bundling reduces transaction and search costs for consumers.

However, bundling may have disadvantages as well in some cases. Consumers may prefer to mix and match components—a common strategy in building home entertainment systems and increasingly popular for music collections. For example, while most consumers are happy to have air conditioning as standard equipment in most automobiles today, perhaps some in colder climates preferred the days when it was an option.[11]

IMPLICATIONS FOR PRODUCT DESIGN. The costs for consumers and firms help explain the products that businesses actually offer from among the many they could offer. Firms have to weigh the demand for a particular product offering against the costs of making it available as a stand-alone product or as part of another product. Many products are not offered at all because there is not enough demand to warrant businesses' incurring the costs of producing and distributing them. Some men would no doubt prefer to get their shoes without shoelaces because they have a favorite shoelace they like to use. But the number is probably so few that it would not pay to offer this option at shoe stores. Other products are offered only separately because few people want them as a system. Although this is changing, many

---

10. Tim Moran, "What's Bugging the High-Tech Car?" *New York Times*, February 6, 2005, p. 14.
11. For a discussion of bundling in automobile packages, see Evans and Salinger (2005, p. 79, note 6).

families buy their own ingredients for dinner rather than prepackaged meals. In other cases there is enough demand for the components and the bundle for producers to offer it both ways.

Consider a simple example. One hundred consumers would pay $10 for A; fifty would pay $6 for B, and ten would pay $20 for AB. It costs $1 to produce each unit of A and B and $2 to produce each unit of AB. Fixed costs are $200 for each of these three products. In this case the unit cost, for meeting all demand, of A is $3, the unit cost of B is $5, and the unit cost of AB is $22. Each component could be provided separately for a profit since the consumer willingness to pay for each unit is greater than the cost of producing each unit ($10 versus $3 for A, and $6 versus $5 for B). However, the bundle cannot be provided profitably because the unit costs exceed what people will pay (it costs $22 to make AB, but consumers will only pay $20). The problem here is lack of demand. Not enough people want the bundle to make it profitable to provide.

Firms sometimes offer pure bundles because even though some consumers do not want portions of the bundle, it is cheaper to sell the components together. To see the intuition, consider the extreme case in which each of several types of consumers wants one component but none of the others. If the fixed costs of providing each of the components is high enough, it pays to combine these together. It is cheaper to give consumers a component they do not want than to provide the component they do want separately. The manufacturer saves money and the consumers often get a lower price than they would otherwise.

A simple example illustrates this. There are two consumers: person 1 is willing to pay $5 for A and nothing for B; person 2 is willing to pay $5 for B for but nothing for A. It costs the manufacturer $2 for A and B separately. The fixed cost of offering a product at all is $1. The manufacturer could sell a unit of A and B separately for $5 each, collect $10 in revenue, incur $4 in manufacturing cost and $2 in product-offering cost, and make a profit of $4. Or it could sell a bundle AB for $5, collect $10 in revenue, incur $4 in manufacturing cost and $1 in product-offering cost, and make a profit of $5. Bundling is the best strategy. In this case the manufacturer pockets the difference, but with competition some of the cost savings would get passed on to the consumer. Moreover, if the fixed cost of offering a product was $5, it would not be profitable to offer A or B (the additional $4 in fixed cost wipes out the profit of $4), but it would be profitable to offer *AB* (the manufacturer would earn $1 of profit). It will be shown later that being able to segment consumers is one of the explanations for this phenomenon. But another explanation—and the one emphasized here—is that the manufacturer can avoid the multiple fixed costs of offering separate products.

It is easy to see from these considerations why firms offer only a fraction of the products—defined by the combination of components—they could. The examples above involve just two components for which there are three possible products. With three components there would be seven possible products (*ABC, AB, AC, BC, A, B, C*); with ten there would be 1,023. Even minimal fixed costs of offering these configurations to distributors or consumers would encourage producers to reduce the number of offerings to those for which there is significant demand. If you think about the products you buy, while you may have a great deal of choice, you have infinitely less than you could have if firms did not bundle components—and things that could in principle be sold separately—together.

Exploiting Demand

Firms bundle components because it enables them to sell more and usually make more profits. That can be true for three demand-related reasons.[12]

COMPLEMENTARY COMPONENTS. The "give away the razor to sell the blades" strategy is famous in business and economics. This approach is profitable because the razor and the blades are complements—a decrease in the price of one increases the demand for the other. In some cases decreasing the price of one component to nothing makes sense. The firm loses money on that component. But it stimulates the demand for the other component on which it does make money. With products that are strong complements, the profits from the positively priced component make up for losses on the zero-priced component.

So far this does not say anything about bundling. But it often saves distribution and packaging costs to sell two goods together. If the firm is giving one away for free anyway, it might as well avail itself of these cost savings. Not surprisingly, razors and blades are usually included in the same package. Consumers benefit from this.

---

12. Adams and Yellen (1976); Bakos and Brynjolfsson (1999).

AGGREGATING ACROSS CONSUMERS. Firms may also find that it pays to bundle even if demands are not complementary. This was demonstrated above: bundling persuaded two consumers to buy a product even though each wanted only a single component. This saved the manufacturer costs.

More generally, businesses can exploit the law of large numbers when they are producing products that have many components.[13] Consumers place different valuations on the various features available to them. You value the arts section of the newspaper highly while your spouse does not care much for it; your spouse values the sports section highly while you do not care much for that section. The valuations for any component can be quite dispersed across consumers with different tastes. If all these components are combined into a single product, the variations tend to cancel each other out. At any given price, there will be more people who will buy the bundle than would buy any component or subset of components.

This of course means that many people are getting components that they do not care for. But if it does not cost much to provide these components and if it is expensive to offer multiple product versions, bundling components together into a single product typically expands demand. These assumptions are especially likely to hold for information goods for which the marginal cost of providing the product (and any component of it) is low, and the costs of developing and distributing the product are high. Newspapers are a good example. They provide many features from crossword puzzles to astrology tables to stock listings to articles on ballet that only a portion of their readers care about. But relative to the cost of producing the newspaper, these features are not that expensive to add. By including them, the newspaper brings in more readers at its typical price, sells more copies, and therefore covers more of the fixed costs of producing the paper. Generally, consumers are better off as a result of such bundling.[14]

PRICE DISCRIMINATION. Despite its name, economists generally view price discrimination as benign or welfare enhancing since it enables firms to increase output and recover fixed costs.[15] Different product combinations

---

13. See Schmalensee (1982); Bakos and Brynjolfsson (1999).

14. Bakos and Brynjolfsson (1999).

15. See the discussion of price discrimination in Carlton and Perloff (2005, pp. 301–08) and Baumol and Swanson (2003). In *Illinois Tool Works*, the Court unanimously held that "similarly, while price

also enable firms to charge different prices to different consumer segments in order to extract more of their willingness to pay. A few of the examples above can be characterized this way although their key feature was that the bundling strategy was driven by the need to cover costs and attract enough consumers.

The idea that bundling can be used to price discriminate dates back to a paper by Nobel prize–winning economist George Stigler. Stigler tried to explain why movie distributors required movie houses to take bundles of pictures.[16] Suppose for movie A exhibitor 1 is willing to pay $8,000 and exhibitor 2, $7,000; for movie B exhibitor 1 is willing to pay $2,500 and exhibitor 2, $3,000. If the movie distributor charges a single price to the two distributors, it would charge $7,000 and $2,500 to attract both exhibitors; the distributor collects $9,500 from each for a total of $19,000. But consider how much the exhibitors would be willing to pay for both movies: exhibitor 1 would pay $10,500 and exhibitor 2 would pay $10,000. Thus if the distributor charged $10,000 for the bundle, it would collect $20,000. It therefore makes more money.

Bundling can be used in a different way. Different groups of consumers place varying values on groups of components. It is possible to design packages that segment these consumers. Some will want the car with the sports package while others will want the basic package. The firm can then charge a premium to groups that have a particularly high demand for a particular package and offer an especially aggressive price to consumers that are very sensitive to price but are also willing to take the no-frills deal. For this to work, there must be a predictable correlation between combinations of components and demand (for example, elastic demand or low demand for frills). A number of studies have found, for example, that automobile companies have much higher markups on luxury models than base models.[17]

---

discrimination may provide evidence of market power, particularly if buttressed by evidence that the patentee has charged an above-market price for the tied package, . . . it is generally recognized that it also occurs in fully competitive markets" (citations omitted).

16. Stigler (1983, chap. 15).

17. Berry, Levinsohn, and Pakes (1995).

Summary: Optimal Product Design and Product Offerings

There is no single explanation as to why businesses offer pure components, mixed bundling, or pure bundling. The most profitable strategy depends on the particular cost and demand situation faced by the firm as well as what the competition is doing. But there are some general tendencies.

Firms offer *pure bundles* of components when

—there is little demand for other combinations of these components relative to the cost of offering them,

—the marginal cost of including components is very low relative to the additional customers that are pulled in, and

—pure bundling is an effective method for appealing to different customer segments.

Firms offer *mixed bundles* when

—there is sufficient demand for a product configuration relative to the cost of offering it and

—different bundled offerings facilitate segmenting customers.

Firms offer *components without any bundles* when

—there is little demand for combining components or consumers can do this themselves very easily and

—the fixed or marginal costs of combining components are prohibitive relative to demand.

Economists have identified circumstances in which firms may not offer the product configurations that are identical to what an all-knowing planner, seeking to maximize social welfare, would do. For example, under certain assumptions firms offer too much product variety and offer bundles that are socially inefficient. Under other assumptions they might not offer bundles that would benefit consumers. But there is no theoretical basis for concluding that there are systematic biases or biases that can be identified, much less corrected, through regulatory intervention.[18] Moreover, these possibilities should not make us lose sight of the fact that bundling of features saves producers and consumers money, provides consumers with products they want, and is often a source of product innovation.

---

18. See Evans and Salinger (2005, note 6). See also Bakos and Brynjolfsson (1999, note 14).

Anticompetitive Tying Can Occur
Only under Special Conditions

Despite its pervasiveness, antitrust courts and regulators have fretted over the anticompetitive use of bundling for many years. Economists have found that there are, at least in theory, situations in which firms could use bundling strategically to harm competition and consumers. But, by and large, economists seem to agree that most concerns about tying are misplaced.

Single-Monopoly Profit Theorem

The famous Chicago School single-monopoly profit theorem shows that under certain assumptions firms with monopoly power in one market do not have the incentive to attempt to extend their monopoly power to other competitive markets. Either price discrimination, which few economists find objectionable, or efficiencies, which of course are applauded, would seem to be more plausible explanations for tying.

Take the case in which a firm has a monopoly in A, and consumers use the monopoly product A and another product B in fixed proportions. Examples include cars and radios, computers and microprocessors, and shoes and shoelaces. The marginal cost of supplying B is c, which equals its price under competitive supply, p_c. Consumers have a final demand for the combined product $A + B$. The monopolist maximizes profit by determining the profit-maximizing price for this combination; that gives the monopolist the most profit it could possibly obtain. The monopolist can achieve this profit in several ways.

—Offer the bundle at a combined price p_c.

—Offer A only at a price $p_c - c$ and have consumers purchase B from competitive suppliers.

—Offer A at a price of $p_c - c$ and B at a price of c along with the other competitive suppliers.

From the monopolist's standpoint, it has nothing to gain by getting a monopoly in B. It would still collect the same monopoly profit based on the combined price of p_c.

Interestingly, the only incentive for the monopolist in this example is to make sure that some firm is selling B competitively. It wants to avoid what economists call the *double monopoly markup* problem.[19] If another firm had a monopoly in *B*, that firm would restrict the output of *B* and raise its price above *c*. That would tend to reduce the sales of *A* and hurt the *A* monopoly's profits. So in this case monopoly *A* has an incentive to create competition in *B*. It might do that, perhaps, by producing *B* itself.

Many products that might be provided as bundles, however, are not used in fixed proportions. For example, fax machines use varying amounts of ink cartridges over time, and people eat varying amounts of bread when they dine. The single-monopoly profit theorem does not necessarily hold when *A* and *B* are used in variable proportions. With varying proportions the monopolist still has incentives to want competitive supply and has limited interest in monopolizing the other product.[20] However, there are possibilities for increasing monopoly profit through bundling with variable proportions that would need to be considered. In many of these cases, however, profits can be increased because bundling facilitates price discrimination. Generally, economists do not look on such price discrimination with disapproval since it can increase social welfare (although it may not).

Acquiring or Maintaining Monopoly through Tying

Not much that economists say is airtight, and the Chicago School–inspired view that tying was benign or efficient is no exception. Economists have identified two scenarios in which monopoly firms have the incentive and the ability to tie their monopoly product *A* to a product *B* that is not a monopoly product. Both cases only apply when *A* and *B* are not used in fixed proportions. The crux of both scenarios is that there are scale economies in the production of *B*. By foreclosing enough demand to competing producers of *B*, the monopolist denies them scale economies and captures the *B* market.[21]

In these cases it is possible to identify situations in which the monopolist finds that it is profitable to tie *B* to *A* to foreclose the market to com-

19. See the discussion of double monopoly markup in Carlton and Perloff (2005, p. 415, note 15).

20. With variable proportions tying can become a means to facilitate price discrimination; however, it should be noted that price discrimination can increase social welfare. See Carlton and Perloff (2005, pp. 306–07; pp. 321–22, note 15).

21. Tirole (2005).

peting B suppliers and to raise the price of B higher than it would be in the absence of this foreclosure, thereby reducing consumer welfare. Carlton and Perloff give the example of a hotel on an island whose guests like to play tennis.[22] By tying the use of the hotel to the use of a tennis club, the hotel can deny enough volume to other tennis clubs and end up with a tennis club monopoly. It will then be able to charge guests and nonguests a higher price for playing tennis.

It is also possible to find situations in which the monopolist finds it beneficial to monopolize the B market because it is possible that the B producers will evolve over time into competitors. Therefore, the monopolist engages in foreclosure to prevent an erosion of its profits in A rather than to obtain profits in B.[23] That was the theory behind the antitrust case against Microsoft involving an Internet browser. Microsoft, the argument went, saw Netscape as a potential software platform rival to Windows. Rather than risk the Netscape browser's evolving into a competitive threat to Windows, Microsoft tried to eliminate Netscape through tying.[24]

Economists who have authored papers identifying these possible anticompetitive uses of tying have been careful to note that they are special cases and that one would need to determine whether the conditions under which they could occur apply in the particular case in question.[25]

Three observations about these theories on the anticompetitive use of tying are worth keeping in mind.

First, the tying strategies used by the would-be monopolist in these theories are costly. The monopolist provides a suboptimal package to consumers (it denies them choices they would like to have) and therefore sacrifices profits. It must weigh these losses against future gains resulting from foreclosure. Second, these tying strategies only work if the monopolist can completely foreclose competition in the tied-good market, or at least substantially reduce it. The success of the strategy, therefore, depends on the existence of barriers to entry into the tied-good market. Finally, foreclosure of competition in the tied-good market does not necessarily lead to lower consumer welfare.

22. Carlton and Perloff (2005, p. 389, note 15).
23. Carlton and Waldman (2002).
24. This is not the place to debate this. However, my views on this can be found in Evans, Nichols, and Schmalensee (2001, 2005).
25. See Carlton and Waldman (2002, p. 215, note 23). See also Whinston (1990).

Loyalty Rebates and Other Complex Pricing Strategies

It is also possible to cause competitive harm through the use of sophisticated pricing strategies. First, it is possible for a firm to offer a mixed bundle but at prices that effectively force consumers to take the tied product. That would be the case if the bundle were substantially cheaper than the sum of the components so that consumers pay less than the competitive price to obtain the tied product. This situation has the same economic effects as the tying case discussed above.

Second, it is possible for a firm to engage in "loyalty rebates" that make it prohibitively expensive for a consumer to buy any component of a bundle from a competitor. For example, suppose a "monopoly" seller gave consumers a 20 percent discount if it purchased 90 percent of its requirements for products A, B, and C from the company. In this case a competing supplier would have difficulty competing for a significant (more than 10 percent) portion of the buyer's business. The buyer would lose the entire 20 percent discount on all of its purchases as a result of falling below the 90 percent threshold.

Whether and under what circumstances loyalty discounts are anticompetitive is a subject of much debate among economists and in the antitrust case law.[26] On the one hand, loyalty and other volume-related discounts lead to lower prices that one does not want to discourage. On the other hand, it is possible that such discounts could preclude entry and sustain a monopoly. Whether the loyalty discounts actually do foreclose competitors is an empirical question that depends on the magnitude of the discounts and the extent to which firms can compete for the entire contract.[27]

So what can be taken from the economics literature on tying? It is possible to identify situations in which tying may be anticompetitive. These situations occur only under particular circumstances, and one would have to verify that those circumstances applied or were plausible in a particular case. In the economics literature, though, there is no support for the view that tying is presumptively bad. In fact the literature finds that tying is presumptively good and that there is little disagreement on this.[28]

---

26. See Spector (2005); Kobayashi (2005); Heimler (2005).
27. Spector (2004); Padilla (2005).
28. See Carlton and Waldman in chapter 3 of this volume.

Jefferson Parish and American Tying Law

Like many unilateral practices, tying has a long and convoluted history in antitrust jurisprudence. One must go back to 1922 to find the first tying violation under U.S. antitrust law. In *United Shoe Machinery Corp.* v. *United States*, the defendant's leases were found to contain tying restrictions that lessened competition.[29] Although the clauses did not explicitly prohibit the use of a competitor's shoe machine, the practical effect of such clauses effectively restricted using a competitor's shoe machinery in combination with United Shoe's machines. United Shoe was found to be in violation of section 3 of the Clayton Antitrust Act of 1914.[30]

A number of significant antitrust cases over the next sixty-two years found that companies had engaged in per se tying violations. The most extreme view of tying expressed on the record was by Justice Felix Frankfurter. He thought that "tying arrangements serve hardly any purpose beyond the suppression of competition."[31]

It was against this backdrop of hostility toward tying that the Supreme Court looked at tying in the 1984 *Jefferson Parish* case. The historical context of the *Jefferson Parish* decision is worth noting. This 1984 decision occurred seven years after the *Sylvania* decision opened the floodgates of Chicago School–influenced reasoning in evaluating antitrust cases.[32] The *Sylvania* decision reversed the long-standing precedent that vertical territorial restraints were a per se violation of the antitrust laws. A few years later,

---

29. 258 U.S. 451 (1922). Before the *United Shoe* case, the first tying violation was discussed in *Motion Picture Patents Co.* v. *Universal Film Manufacturing Co.* in 1917, which overruled *Henry* v. *A.B. Dick Co.* However, both cases were tried under patent infringement law and not antitrust law. In *Motion Picture Patents*, the patent holder on a movie projector sold projectors to theaters with the agreement that the theaters would only project movies supplied by the plaintiff or its designees. After a theater did not abide by the agreement to only exhibit authorized movies, the plaintiff sued for patent infringement, but the Supreme Court held that movie films were not part of the patented movie projector, and thus no patent infringement had occurred. See *Motion Picture Patents Co.* v. *Universal Film Manufacturing Co.*, 243 U.S. 502 (1917); *Henry* v. *A.B. Dick Co.*, 224 U.S. 1 (1912).

30. Tying was first found to be a violation of section 1 of the Sherman Act in *International Salt Co.* v. *United States*, 332 U.S. 392 (1947). The *International Salt* case focused on a company that was the largest U.S. producer of industrial salt. The salt company owned patents on two salt machines and conditioned the lease of these machines on the requirement that the lessee purchase all salt used in the leased machines from the appellant salt company. The Court held that such a requirement violated section 1 of the Sherman Act and section 3 of the Clayton Act because the agreements tended to create a monopoly and because it is per se unreasonable to exclude competition from a substantial market.

31. See *Standard Oil Co.* v. *United States*, 337 U.S. 293, 305 (1949).

32. *Continental T.V.* v. *GTE Sylvania*, 433 U.S. 36 (1977).

the scope of the per se rule was curtailed even further when in the *BMI* case the Supreme Court ruled that even some price fixing arrangements may have efficiency justifications that would warrant their analysis under the rule of reason.[33] Then, in *Matsushita* (1986) and *Brooke Group* (1993), the Supreme Court adopted Chicago School reasoning in raising the hurdles that plaintiffs faced in bringing, under the rule of reason, predatory pricing cases.[34]

After *Sylvania* the Supreme Court shifted almost all practices except hard-core cartel behavior into the rule of reason category and infused economic analysis into the rule of reason inquiries for virtually all practices. In *Jefferson Parish*, however, the Supreme Court left tying in a peculiar per se box in which tying would be automatically condemned if it flunked a new test.

Jefferson Parish Hospital, outside New Orleans, entered into an exclusive agreement with a group of anesthesiologists to provide anesthesiology services at the hospital. When a doctor scheduled his patient for surgery at the hospital, he had to pick—or recommend to the patient—one of these anesthesiologists. A competing group of anesthesiologists claimed that Jefferson Parish Hospital was engaging in an anticompetitive tie in violation of section 1 of the Sherman Act.

The district court rejected the per se approach in favor of a rule of reason analysis of this case. The lower court ruled the plaintiff could not prevail on a per se analysis because he had not made the necessary demonstration that the hospital "dominated" the market for its services. Then, under a rule of reason analysis, the court found that defendant hospital did not violate section 1 of the Sherman Act by excluding Dr. Edwin G. Hyde (plaintiff) from its medical staff because the anticompetitive effects of its closed group policy were few and far outweighed by the many benefits to patient care.[35]

The Court of Appeals for the Fifth Circuit reversed the district court's judgment. It found that a per se approach was appropriate for the case. In particular it rejected the hospital's explanation for why the tie led to efficiencies.[36] The Supreme Court agreed to hear an appeal.

33. *Broadcast Music, Inc.* v. *Columbia Broadcasting System, Inc.*, 441 U.S. 1 (1979).

34. *Matsushita Elec. Industrial Co.* v. *Zenith Radio*, 475 U.S. 574 (1986); *Brooke Group* v. *Brown and Williamson Tobacco Co.*, 509 U.S. 209 (1993).

35. *Dr. Edwin G. Hyde* v. *Jefferson Parish Hospital District No. 2*, 513 F. Supp. 532 (E.D. La., 1981).

36. *Dr. Edwin G. Hyde* v. *Jefferson Parish Hospital District No. 2*, 686 F.2d 286 (5th Circuit, 1982).

The Court wrestled with what to do about tying. A five-judge majority was troubled by the sweeping condemnation of tying in the previous case law.[37] But the Court was hesitant to overturn such a long-standing body of jurisprudence. Justice Brennan noted in a separate concurring opinion that

> it may, for example, be entirely innocuous that the seller exploits its control over the tying product to "force" the buyer to purchase the tied product. For when the seller exerts market power only in the tying-product market, it makes no difference to him or his customers whether he exploits that power by raising the price of the tying product or by "forcing" customers to buy a tied product. On the other hand, tying may make the provision of packages of goods and services more efficient. A tie-in should be condemned only when its anti-competitive impact outweighs its contribution to efficiency.[38]

The majority also noted that "it is clear, however, that not every refusal to sell two products separately can be said to restrain competition."[39] But "it is far too late in the history of our antitrust jurisprudence to question the proposition that certain tying arrangements pose an unacceptable risk of stifling competition and therefore are unreasonable 'per se.'"[40]

The Court came up with a new test, described below. Applying this test, it found that there was no anticompetitive tie. Justice Sandra Day O'Connor, along with Chief Justice Warren Burger and Justices Lewis Powell and William Rehnquist, agreed with the Court's decision to reverse the appeals court. But O'Connor argued that the case was properly analyzed under the rule of reason. She noted that

> the per se label in the tying context has generated more confusion than coherent law because it appears to invite lower courts to omit the

---

37. Justice John Stevens delivered the opinion of the court, in which Justices William Brennan, Byron White, Thurgood Marshall, and Harry Blackmun joined. Justice Brennan filed a concurring opinion, in which Justice Marshall joined. Note that Justice Stevens is also the author of the 2006 *Illinois Works* decision. That decision rejects the presumption that a patent confers market power for the purpose of assessing tying and expresses some skepticism over the evolution of the Court's jurisprudence on tying.

38. *Jefferson Parish Hospital Dist. No. 2* v. *Hyde*, 466 U.S. 2, 41 (1984).

39. *Jefferson Parish Hospital Dist. No. 2* v. *Hyde*, 11.

40. *Jefferson Parish Hospital Dist. No. 2* v. *Hyde*, 9.

analysis of economic circumstances of the tie that has always been a necessary element of tying analysis. The time has therefore come to abandon the "per se" label and refocus the inquiry on the adverse economic effects, and the potential economic benefits, that the tie may have.[41]

The majority came up with what they saw as a compromise between the draconian view of tying taken by their predecessors and their desire to keep some semblance of a per se rule.[42] They found that tying was per se illegal if there were two separate products, for which the firm had market power in the tying product and for which the tie affected a not insubstantial portion of interstate commerce. To determine whether products were separate, the majority decision said that one should look at whether the two products could exist in separate product markets with their own sufficient demand. Specifically, the court stated,

> The answer to the question whether petitioners have utilized a tying arrangement must be based on whether there is a possibility that the economic effect of the arrangement is that condemned by the rule against tying—that petitioners have foreclosed competition on the merits in a product market distinct from the market for the tying item. Thus in this case no tying arrangement can exist unless there is a sufficient demand for the purchase of anesthesiological services separate from hospital services to identify a distinct product market in which it is efficient to offer anesthesiological services separately from hospital services.[43]

Moreover, whether two products are considered separate products is not a function of whether the two products are complements or not. Specifically, the court stated, "Our cases indicate, however, that the answer to the question whether one or two products are involved turns not on the functional relation between them but rather on the character of the demand for the two items."[44]

41. *Jefferson Parish Hospital Dist. No. 2* v. *Hyde*, 34–36.
42. See Areeda and Hovenkamp (1996).
43. *Jefferson Parish Hospital Dist. No. 2* v. *Hyde*, 222.
44. *Jefferson Parish Hospital Dist. No. 2* v. *Hyde*, 19.

Applying this test to the facts at hand, the majority decision found that anesthesiology and surgical services were separate products and that there was sufficient demand to offer anesthesiology services separately. But they also found that Jefferson Parish Hospital lacked market power.

This denouement highlights the peculiarity of the test. On the one hand, the majority, following the appeals court, seemed to reject various explanations the hospital gave as to why it wanted a dedicated team of anesthesiologists. On the other hand, the majority found that the hospital did not have significant market power, which implies that tying could not have been an anticompetitive strategy. Thus the majority was left with no plausible explanation for why the hospital engaged in tying.

Tying: Poster Child for Antitrust Modernization

As of 2005 very few practices really fall under per se condemnation. These include hard-core cartels that fix minimum prices. Since *BMI* it has been possible for groups of firms to persuade the courts to evaluate price fixing under the rule of reason if there is a plausible efficiency explanation. Among unilateral practices only minimum resale price maintenance is per se illegal. In *Sylvania* in 1977 and *Khan* in 1997, the Supreme Court reversed earlier decisions that had treated nonprice vertical restraints and maximum resale price maintenance as per se illegal.[45]

Jefferson Parish left tying as a rather incompletely evolved species of unilateral practices. The decision made it easier for the defendant to request dismissal of a tying claim than did the previous case law. The percentage of tying claims that were dismissed by federal district courts increased significantly in the two decades after *Jefferson Parish* compared to the preceding two decades (see table 4-2). So the Supreme Court imparted its increasingly skeptical view of the anticompetitive nature of unilateral practices of tying.

Tying cases, however, continue apace. Between 2000 and 2005, more than sixty cases involving an antitrust tying claim were filed in federal courts. Indeed, the largest settlement in antitrust history—in the retailers' case against MasterCard and Visa—came on the heels of a district court decision

45. *Continental T.V.* v. *GTE Sylvania*, 36; *State Oil Company* v. *Barkat U. Khan*, 118 S. Ct. 275 (1997).

Table 4-2. *Outcome of Summary Judgment Motions to Dismiss Tying Claim, 1964-2005*[a]

Period	Granted	Denied	Percent granted
1964–84 (pre–*Jefferson Parish*)	184	46	68.66
1984–2005 (post–*Jefferson Parish*)	246	36	80.92

Source: Author's calculations based on data collected from Lexis-Nexis.

a. Ideally I would have liked to examine outcomes of all tying cases in the U.S. federal district courts. However, the Lexis database contains only cases in which the court issued an opinion. It does not contain comprehensive information on cases that went to jury trials. The majority of court opinions obtained were issued when a party moved for summary judgment. Therefore, the cases shown here are limited to those that focused on a motion for summary judgment filed by the defendant.

that found that *Jefferson Parish* was the proper standard.[46] The lower court ruled, as a matter of law, that the card associations failed all of the prongs of the test. It left open the possibility that the plaintiffs had to prove competitive harm to a jury.[47]

In the last twenty years, U.S. antitrust law has made enormous strides toward becoming intellectually coherent and based on sound economic analysis. In many ways it has become boring, in part because there are relatively few disagreements among economists on the right approach (as distinct from the application to a particular set of facts). Among enforcement agencies and in the courts, economic analysis now plays a preeminent role in bringing and evaluating cases. To the extent there is disagreement, it surrounds unilateral practices.

The debate, however, concerning unilateral practices concerns mainly how to conduct the rule of reason analysis. Should the profit-sacrifice test be used to distinguish predatory from nonpredatory actions?[48] To what extent should the courts insist on evidence of consumer harm or infer consumer harm from the nature of the practice?[49] Should bundled rebates be subject to a full-blown rule of reason analysis or subjected to something like the *Brooke Group* test?

46. *In re Visa Check/Mastermoney Antitrust Litigation*, 2003 U.S. Dist LEXIS 4965 (E.D. N.Y., 2003).

47. For more on competitive harm, see *Dr. Edwin G. Hyde* v. *Jefferson Parish Hospital District No. 2*, 513 F. Supp. 532 (E.D. La. 1981).

48. See *Verizon Communications Inc.* v. *Law Offices of Curtis V. Trinko, LLP*, 540 U.S. 398 (2004); Elhauge (2003); White (2005); Melamed (2005); Salop (2005).

49. See Chang, Evans, and Schmalensee (2003); Muris (2005).

There is no serious debate that unilateral practices should be subjected to a per se test rather than a rule of reason analysis. Likewise, there is no debate among economists or legal scholars that tying should be removed from the genus of unilateral practices and placed in its own leper colony. In the last decade, there have been roughly 100 articles concerning tying in peer-reviewed economics journals and law reviews in the United States. Only one advocated the per se treatment of tying.[50] Moreover, not a single economist or antitrust scholar has offered a serious defense of the *Jefferson Parish* test. More than a quarter century ago Justice O'Connor said,

> The time has therefore come to abandon the "per se" label and refocus the inquiry on the adverse economic effects, and the potential economic benefits, that the tie may have. The law of tie-ins will thus be brought into accord with the law applicable to all other allegedly anticompetitive economic arrangements, except those few horizontal or quasi-horizontal restraints that can be said to have no economic justification whatsoever. This change will rationalize rather than abandon tie-in doctrine as it is already applied.[51]

Modern antitrust analysis does not support the per se condemnation of tying or the *Jefferson Parish* test. Neither should modern antitrust law. Ending the per se treatment of tying—and the *Jefferson Parish* compromise— would be a fitting and deserving tribute to Justice O'Connor.

50. See Campbell (2002).
51. *Jefferson Parish Hospital Dist. No. 2* v. *Hyde*, 34–35.

References

Adams, William J., and Janet L. Yellen. 1976. "Commodity Bundling and the Burden of Monopoly." *Quarterly Journal of Economics* 90, no. 3: 475–98.

Areeda, Philip E., and Herbert Hovenkamp. 1996. *Antitrust Law: An Analysis of Antitrust Principles and Their Application*, vol. 5, pp. 29–33. New York: Aspen Publishers.

Bakos, Yannis, and Eric Brynjolfsson. 1999. "Bundling Information Goods: Pricing, Profits, and Efficiency." *Management Science* 45, no. 12: 1613–30.

Baumol, William, and Daniel Swanson. 2003. "The New Economy and Ubiquitous Competitive Price Discrimination: Identifying Defensible Criteria of Market Power." *Antitrust Law Journal* 70, no. 3: 661–85.

Berry, Steven, James Levinsohn, and Ariel Pakes. 1995. "Automobile Prices in Market Equilibrium." *Econometrica* 60, no. 4: 889–917.

Campbell, Christopher P. 2002. "Fit to Be Tied: How *United States* v. *Microsoft Corp.* Incorrectly Changed the Standard for Sherman Act Tying Violations Concerning Software." *Loyola of Los Angeles Entertainment Law Review* 22, no. 3: 583–612.

Carlton, Dennis W., and Jeffrey M. Perloff. 2005. *Modern Industrial Organization.* 4th ed. Boston, Mass.: Addison-Wesley.

Carlton, Dennis W., and Michael Waldman. 2002. "The Strategic Use of Tying to Preserve and Create Market Power in Evolving Industries." *RAND Journal of Economics* 33, no. 2: 194–220.

Chang, Howard, David Evans, and Richard Schmalensee. 2003. "Has the Consumer Harm Standard Lost Its Teeth?" In *High Stakes Antitrust—The Last Hurrah?* edited by Robert W. Hahn, pp. 72–116. Washington: American Enterprise Institute.

Elhauge, Einer. 2003. "Defining Better Monopolization Standards." *Stanford Law Review* 56, no. 2: 253–344.

Evans, David, Albert Nichols, and Richard Schmalensee. 2001. "An Analysis of the Government's Economic Case in *U.S.* v. *Microsoft.*" *Antitrust Bulletin* 46, no. 2: 163–251.

———. 2005. "*U.S.* v. *Microsoft*: Did Consumers Win?" Working Paper 11727. Cambridge, Mass.: National Bureau of Economic Research (October 2005).

Evans, David S., and Michael Salinger. 2004. "The Role of Cost in Determining When Firms Offer Bundles and Ties." Working Paper. (ssrn.com/abstract=555818 [March 2006]).

———. 2005. "Why Do Firms Bundle and Tie? Evidence from Competitive Markets and Implications for Tying Law." *Yale Journal on Regulation* 22, no. 1: 37–89.

Heimler, Alberto. 2005. "Below-Cost Pricing and Loyalty-Inducing Discounts: Are They Restrictive and, If So, When?" *Competition Policy International* 1, no. 2: 149–72.

Kobayashi, Bruce H. 2005. "The Economics of Loyalty Discounts and Antitrust Law in the United States." *Competition Policy International* 1 (Autumn): 115–48.

Melamed, A. Douglas. 2005. "Exclusionary Conduct under the Antitrust Laws: Balancing, Sacrifice, and Refusals to Deal." *Berkeley Technology Law Journal* 20, no. 2: 1247–67.

Muris, Timothy. 2005. "Principles for a Successful Competition Agency." *University of Chicago Law Review* 72 (Winter): 165–87.

Padilla, Jorge. 2005. "Rebates: Efficiency v. Foreclosure. An Economic Commentary." Paper presented at the UCL Antitrust and Regulation Series, University College London, April 26.

Rey, Patrick, Paul Seabright, and Jean Tirole. 2001 (revised 2002). "The Activities of a Monopoly Firm in Adjacent Competitive Markets: Economic Consequences and Implications for Competition Policy." Working Paper 132. Toulouse, France: Institut d'Economie Industrielle.

Salinger, Michael A. 2005. "Challenges in Identifying Anticompetitive Dominant Firm Behavior." Speech before the National Economic Research Associates 2005 Antitrust and Trade Regulation Seminar, Santa Fe, New Mexico, July 7 (www.ftc.gov/speeches/salinger/050711santefe.pdf [March 2006]).

Salop, Steve. 2005. "Consumer Welfare Effects and the Flawed Profit-Sacrifice Standard. Georgetown University Law Center.

Schmalensee, Richard. 1982. "Commodity Bundling by Single-Product Monopolies." *Journal of Law and Economics* 25 (April): 67–71.

Seabright, Paul. 2002. "Tying and Bundling: From Economics to Competition Policy." Paper presented at the Centre for the New Europe Market Insights Event, Brussels, Belgium, September 19.

Spector, David. 2004. "Loyalty Rebates and Related Pricing Practices: When Should Competition Authorities Worry?" In *Global Competition Policy: Economic Issues and Impacts*, edited by David S. Evans and Jorge Padilla, pp. 317–48. Emeryville, Calif.: LECG.

———. 2005. "Loyalty Rebates: An Assessment of Competition Concerns and a Proposed Structured Rule of Reason." *Competition Policy International* 1, no. 2: 89–113.

Stigler, George J. 1983. *The Organization of Industry*. University of Chicago Press.

Tirole, Jean. 2005. "The Analysis of Tying Cases: A Primer." *Competition Policy International* 1, no. 1: 1–25.

Whinston, Michael D. 1990. "Tying, Foreclosure, and Exclusion." *American Economic Review* 80, no. 4: 837–59.

White, Barbara Ann. 2005. "Evolving Antitrust Treatment of Dominant Firms: Choosing among Antitrust Liability Standards under Incomplete Information: Assessments of and Aversions to the Risk of Being Wrong." *Berkeley Technology Law Journal* 20, no. 2: 1173–84.

Contributors

DENNIS W. CARLTON
Graduate School of Business
University of Chicago

DAVID S. EVANS
LECG and
Faculty of Laws
University College London

ROBERT W. HAHN
AEI-Brookings Joint Center for Regulatory Studies

BRUCE H. KOBAYASHI
George Mason University School of Law

MICHAEL WALDMAN
Johnson Graduate School of Management
Cornell University

Index

JOINT CENTER

AEI-BROOKINGS JOINT CENTER FOR REGULATORY STUDIES